BOOKS BY JAY LEACH

How Should We Then Live

Behold the Man

The Blood Runs Through It

Drawn Away

Give Me Jesus

A Lamp unto My Feet

Grace that Saves

The Narrow Way

Radical Restoration of the Church

Manifestation of the True Children of God

According to Pattern

Battle Cry

Is there not a Cause?

We Would See Jesus

According to Pattern 2nd Edition

The Apostolic Rising

For His Glory

Where Have All the Shepherds Gone?

WHERE
HAVE ALL THE
SHEPHERDS
GONE?

GOD IS RESTORING HIS CHURCH TO ITS FORMER POWER AND GLORY!

"A study guide is located at the end of each chapter."

Jay Leach

Order this book online at www.trafford.com
or email orders@trafford.com

Most Trafford titles are also available at major online book retailers.

Print information available on the last page.

ISBN: 978-1-6987-1096-9 (sc)
ISBN: 978-1-6987-1095-2 (e)

Library of Congress Control Number: 2022902252

Because of the dynamic nature of the Internet, any web addresses or links contained in
this book may have changed since publication and may no longer be valid. The views
expressed in this work are solely those of the author and do not necessarily reflect the
views of the publisher, and the publisher hereby disclaims any responsibility for them.

Any people depicted in stock imagery provided by Getty Images are models, and such images are
being used for illustrative purposes only.
Certain stock imagery © Getty Images.

ESV
Unless otherwise indicated, all scripture quotations are from The Holy Bible,
English Standard Version® (ESV®). Copyright ©2001 by Crossway Bibles, a
division of Good News Publishers. Used by permission. All rights reserved.

NKJV
Scripture quotations marked NKJV are taken from the New King James Version.
Copyright © 1982 by Thomas Nelson, Inc. Used by permission. All rights reserved.

NCV
Scripture quotations marked "NCV" are taken from the New Century
Version, Copyright © 1987, 1988, 1991 by Word Publishing, a division of
Thomas Nelson, Inc. Used by permission. All rights reserved.

ESV
Unless otherwise indicated, all scripture quotations are from The Holy Bible,
English Standard Version® (ESV®). Copyright ©2001 by Crossway Bibles, a
division of Good News Publishers. Used by permission. All rights reserved.

NIV
Scripture quotations marked NIV are taken from the Holy Bible, New International
Version®. NIV®. Copyright © 1973, 1978, 1984 by International Bible Society.
Used by permission of Zondervan. All rights reserved. [Biblica]

Trafford rev. 02/04/2022

 www.trafford.com

North America & international
toll-free: 844-688-6899 (USA & Canada)
fax: 812 355 4082

CONTENTS

THE GLORY OF THE SHEPHERD

DEDICATION

"Shepherd the flock of God which is among you, serving as overseers, not by compulsion but willingly, not for dishonest gain but eagerly; nor as being lords over those entrusted to you, but being examples for the flock; and when the Chief Shepherd appears, you will receive the crown of glory that does not fade away" (I Peter 5:2-4).

In every generation God by His sovereign purpose and his powerful plans, raises up some "Issachar(s)." An Issachar is someone who has tapped into the heart and mind of God and understands the times and knows what to do (see 1 Chron. 12:32).

INTRODUCTION

"There is a CRISIS in the American Church!" Books like this always begin by sounding the alarm. Well! Here, it's a shepherding crisis or to be more precise, the failure to shepherd crisis. Long before COVID-19, many of the local Churches in this country were on life support. Christians were leaving churches with hurt and bitter hearts, and some left in order to maintain their spirituality (a major threat today). At the same time, for various reasons many of our local churches did not have a viable prayer ministry or discipleship ministry because at some point to them, these ministries were considered antiquated, inconvenient, not needed and eliminated.

Therefore, many young Christians are being discipled by television, zoom, face book, U-tube and other media, fleshy events, and false theology; because churches have neglected their *primary* responsibility to "make disciples," and teach, practice, and promote the New Covenant formulated by God, a divine agreement and plan between God the Father, and Jesus, the Son to *recover a lost humanity from the devil's power.* The heavenly Father was not willing to lose His beloved creation to the powers of hell! So He formed a *plan of redemption,* and *reconciliation,* one that came completely from His heart of love – before the world was created! Hopefully, this book will be a "shepherd's call and revelation" to all the Church *in* Christ.

Please, be reminded that discipleship is the primary platform instituted by God in His mission to reconcile and grow people (through transformation) into the image of His Son. However, I am sure you will agree – the Church is losing ground in major areas especially the work of God's eternal purposes beginning with His New Covenant[1] (see Psalm 89:34; Ezekiel 18:30-32; Hebrews 8:8-13; 10:16-17) without which, the Great Commandment and the Great Commission has been declared optional by the "carnal" hearts and hands of humanity:

> And He said to him, *"You shall love the Lord your God with all your heart and with all your soul and with all your mind"*[2] (Matthew 22:37 ESV).

> And Jesus came and said unto them, *"All authority in heaven and on earth has been given to me. Go therefore and make disciples of all nations, baptizing them in the name of the Father and of the Son and of the Holy Spirit, teaching them to observe all that I have commanded you. And behold, I am with you always, even to the end of the age"*[3] (Matthew 28:18-20 ESV).

Jesus agreed with God's plan of redemption in the Covenant which required Him to receive a body from the Father in which He would come to earth and shed His life's blood to redeem and reconcile

---

[1] The New Covenant

[2] The Great Commandment

[3] The Great Commission

sinful humanity back to the Father. Throughout history, man has attempted to hide, modify, or deny the New Covenant and our Divine substitute, Jesus Christ, and His death on the cross to rescue us! And the Father who kept His *Covenant promises* to His Son has promised an eternal oath to do the same "for us." Jesus affirmed this part of the Covenant (see John 17:20-26).

Research shows that approximately one quarter of the world professes Christianity, while another quarter Muslim, a quarter Hindu and the final quarter Buddhism, and innumerable beliefs, cults, and minor religions. Additionally, it shows that Muslims and Hindus are doubling in size each year. However, in many areas Christianity has slowed to zero growth during the entire year (2020). Today, we stand on the brink of a new year of opportunities to get it right (2022), if the Lord tarries.

We know that some churches are meeting goals and making progress, but there seems to be something terribly wrong with our *methods or strategies* for reaching the world. It is apparent from the results shown above, after 2000 years with the commands from Christ, the Head, concerning the New Covenant, Great Commandment, and the Great Commission, only ¼ of the world has been Christianized – this cannot be what God intended for His Church! In His prayer, Jesus prays that they might be *sanctified*, that is, set apart *"for the ministry of truth"* (see John 17:17-19). Emphasis is mine throughout.

Another very common crisis is people make a confession of faith and actively participate in the life of the church for a season, before dropping out and returning to their rebellious and loose lifestyle. Often after abandoning the Church and no one knows where the person has gone, and in a number of cases, *don't care*, however, their name remains on the church roll.

Many times, just before death God places them back on the doorstep of the Church. Frequently, their condition through sickness or some other malady is too brief for pastoral intervention with the dying person to find out how he or she stood before God. The person is funeralized. Afterward, that individual must stand before the judgment seat of Christ to give account for his or her life – but before that same throne the shepherd pastors of the flock at the deceased brother or sister's home church will have to give account for this one *lost* sheep.

More of the churches are accepting the world's view that Christianity and the church are components of religion (earthly) and therefore, subject to their inadequate leadership, philosophies, psychology, lusts, and the speculation of legalism; rather than *being* (spiritual) and (supernatural) as clearly recorded in the Bible. Slowly and subtly, many churches have let Christianity devolve into just another set of special days, rules, regulations, practices, and scientific theories to observe. Once again, the church has disregarded what God requires and have simply given Him what they *feel* is fair to give Him [*a mixture of law and grace*] rather than: "The just shall live by faith" (Gal. 3:11 NKJV).

Christ *came down* and established the Church through His blood and His life, then gave His New Covenant people (both Jew and Gentile together) of faith, the privilege of participating in His divine plan (see Hebrews 8:6; 9:14-15). Jesus declared His intention to build His Church (see Matthew 16:18) and the New Testament describes its formation as God's Covenant people, *Spiritual Israel (seed),* who are spiritually united to "meet together," as is the habit of some, and encouraging one another (Hebrews 10:25 ESV). Research shows some an abundance of religions, and different variations in the U.S. are of the devil as they attempt to *reach up* supposedly to God – but He has already reached down to humanity in the New Covenant. Christianity is radically different from every religion in the world. Christianity is Christ and the ending [ian] means [I am nothing]!

There are two ways we can handle sin: **1)** In religion (humanity) *buries* sin, but it can be dug up, and **2)** In the New Covenant (God) forgives and *washes away* sin with the blood of Jesus. Praise God! Humanity can't find it! Jay Leach

Paul further clarified the identity of the New Covenant and the Church, *"to you who have been made holy **in** Christ Jesus. You were called to be God's holy people with all people everywhere who pray in the name of the Lord Jesus Christ, their Lord and ours"* (1 Corinthians 1:2 NCV). Emphasis added. This defines the Church as God's New Covenant people who are distinguished by their common faith in Jesus Christ and their submission to Him as Lord.

The church is also identified in the passage as a local gathering of believers in relation to all disciples globally "everywhere." God's Covenant community of those who are locally assembled and globally united by a common faith in Jesus Christ (the body of Christ). *This is who we are, the Church – the Body of Jesus Christ!*

In obedience to His command the Church, the instrument He commissioned to reconcile a lost world to Himself – is committed to faithfully execute His Great Commission to make disciples. Dietrich Bonhoeffer said, "Christianity without discipleship is always Christianity without Christ."[4] Additionally, the Scripture explains explicitly that our existence as the Church: First and foremost, exists for the glory of God and Christ, who is the Head of the Church (His Body). Paul's letter to the Ephesians is summarized in this verse of praise: *"To Him be glory in the church and in Christ Jesus throughout all generations, forever and ever Amen"* (Ephesians 3:21 ESV).

Through the COVID-19 epidemic, along with its variants, I pray that we all have seen [biblically] the need for [ingathering the

---

[4] Dietrich Bonhoeffer, *The Cost of Discipleship* (New York Macmillan, 1949) 62

church] (see Hebrews 10:25). We need someone! Therefore, we seldom go it alone in isolation! In fact, just today, there were several medical professionals in the news speaking against "isolation." Many who use to assemble each Sunday by tradition in services have chosen to leave the church and go virtual, which really amplifies the isolation problem. In the world, daily we see gyms, other workout clubs, workplaces, places of leisure, and packs of men and women running together. Not only are we social beings, but we also need encouragement when discipline is involved. The apostle Peter, admonishes us that our corporate ministries should be fashioned and our individual spiritual gifts, should function!

If you ask individual Christians today what it means *practically,* to make disciples, sadly, you will likely get mixed and shallow answers or in some cases just blank stares. Where did we get the authority to have exempted "one another" from *any* personal responsibility to "*fish for men?*" I believe most Christians would not say their purpose in life is to make disciples of all nations.

Biblically speaking, isn't *every* single disciple of Jesus Christ intended to make disciples to Him?"

From the very moment the command came out of Jesus' mouth hasn't following Christ involved fishing for men, women, girls, and boys?" Early disciples of Jesus made other disciples not because they had to, but because they desired to! So, what is stopping us from obeying the command today? We need less leaders and more Spirit-filled shepherd pastors, as instructed in the New Covenant. It is our very life! "*In order that in everything God may be glorified through Jesus Christ. To Him belong glory and dominion forever and ever Amen*" (1 Peter 4:11 ESV).

Jay Leach, In His Service,
Fayetteville, NC

SECTION ONE
RESTORING THE CHURCH OF JESUS CHRIST

> "*That He may send Jesus Christ, who was preached to you before, whom heaven must receive until the times of restoration of all things, which God has spoken by the mouth of His holy prophets since the world began*" (Acts 4:20-21 NKJV).

CHAPTER ONE

And afterward, I will pour out My Spirit on all people. Your sons and daughters will prophesy, your old men will dream dreams, your young men will see visions. Even on My servants, both men and women, I will pour out My Spirit in those days. I will show wonders in the heavens and on the earth, blood and fire and billows of smoke (Joel 2:28-30 NIV).

As stated in the introduction, the majority of Christians today are being discipled by popular media, large flashy events, and false theology because local churches have by choice or simply neglected their responsibility to make (spiritually mature) disciples. Yet, the Church is the primary entity God uses to grow people to maturity (discipleship) in Christ Jesus. Many pastors are hired with the focus on growing crowds instead of growing disciples. Our problem then is a lack of maturing disciples (voluntary disobedience). This tells us: that we are not too deep as some claim, but we are too shallow! Perhaps the church should think about what it means to go deeper with fewer people rather than going wider with many. I remember a pastor remarking, that he couldn't wait for things to get back to normal. His friend remarked, "I don't think we will ever return to the pre-quarantine normal." Many are like that pastor – not realizing that that world no longer exists. While there will be challenges, I believe there will be more opportunities – and remember, the quarantine did not catch God by surprise! The pandemic was a wake-up call; to make necessary positive changes to move the church forward.

My hope in writing this book is to present a paradigm that will help local churches implement methods and strategic ministry that will grow spiritually mature, deep, and holistic disciples – to engage the enemy in the battle for the heart and soul of American Church. We are seeing more prayer and discipleship in ministry outside of the local churches because they are so neglected inside. Undoubtedly, much of what is done in many local churches is completely apart from Jesus. We have a chance to get back on our Christ assigned missions. Nevertheless, the fact remains that Jesus commissioned every local church specifically, to reach, teach, form, and holistically develop "spiritually mature followers" of Christ (disciples) until He comes back! I see the Lord using this opportunity to move His church back to center. Are you excited and ready?

Bridging the Gaps

There are gaps in the lives of many people, even among church folk between where they are and where they want to be. In listening to many of those who have left their local churches; their claim is that the churches offer traditional programs and solutions that actually drive people away rather than keep them, for example:

- The pastor (shepherd) is not feeding the sheep (people), the truth of God's Word.
- The church does not feel like a place where a person can be honest about real struggles, issues, and sins.
- Certain sins are acceptable to discuss in church, while other sins are not.
- The church uses shame and guilt in their attempt to motivate behavioral change in people.
- Many people in the local church come across as fakes and/ or unauthentic (unreal).
- The church tries to answer questions that no one is asking.
- To accept church, a person must invest a lot of time, effort and resources in image management or giving the impression that one is doing great and living right, even when it is not true.
- The church is always asking for money.

That means leaders are supposed to bridge the gap. Churches that want to create a culture of deep mature discipleship *must* call on every single member to participate in this dual mission (evangelism), and (the building up the body of Christ). Paul insists that the purpose of the local church is not only to equip the saints for ministry but to *shepherd lead* them in growing in their faith and knowledge of the Son of God (deeper discipleship) "to the measure of the stature of the fullness of Christ" (Ephesians 4:13 ESV).

One of the most disheartening behaviors we see during this season of spiritual conflict is more and more local church cultures are looking to secular models, resources and methodology (in training the laity) within the four walls, rather than through the Bible [biblical model]. This causes the churches to be weak as they attempt to operate, many striving [in the flesh] to do so *without* the power of the Holy Spirit and His gifts and ministries.

Not only that, but Satan has access to get his own unholy children of darkness [his intentionally unsaved children] into the churches through their earthly specialties, abilities, and natural talents. His intent of disrupting and drawing the people "back into the flesh" or [blatant carnality]. In such cases, the primary mission of "making disciples" becomes a (be like me ministry) nil and none.

Some offer the argument of the church being too deep is really trivial, in reality, the church is too shallow. Therefore, we have settled for a shallow approach to discipleship – believing that breadth will lead to depth.

> We are treating this malady of shallowness or not "making disciples" by focusing on shepherding people – but if they want to grow up in Christ; what many of the local churches have to offer is inadequate. Making disciples is a command to the church from our Lord and Savior Jesus Christ not a suggestion! There is no "wiggle room!" – Jay Leach

It has been said, "So many churches have adopted philosophies of ministry that focus on entertainment and growing crowds – instead of growing matured Disciples! Jesus said, "Where two or three come together in My name there am I with them " (Matthew 18:20 NIV). The *promise of Jesus's* **presence** also has a larger application, but it immediately applies to decisions in matters of church discipline (see I Corinthians 5:4). Hopefully, as we continue to experience the fluctuation with Covid-19 and the variants, I pray that our pastors and churches will consider what it means *to go deeper with fewer people* instead of wider with the masses. Perhaps doing so will change our thinking from how to *keep* people to how to *form* them.

At the outset, many in the local churches cannot separate their faith from institutional religion or revelation from speculation, nor can they contemplate a God larger than their experience of Him in their Church tradition. I began ministering in the church more than forty years ago while a career soldier in the US Army. The church has been my world practically all my life. I love the church. However, a couple of decades ago I found it difficult to feel at ease there because it lacks spiritual purpose and missional vitality.

The church is seriously handicapped by the belief that the *test of salvation* is *doctrinal* rather than *behavioral*. Let us have a look as we divide the congregation into two groups:

1. We have one group of the congregation that is engaged in church activity but have not repented of their sin and have decided not to follow Jesus. Jesus defines belief as following Him (see Luke 9:23-25).

2. Those in the second group have truly repented of their sin and in good faith are following Jesus – but in many cases, what it means to follow Jesus has been reduced to church attendance, financial giving, and serving on a board, committee, and music ministries.

Neither of these conditions happen with a conscious choice; but happen by customs and traditional church culture. In the first group we have people who are religious but lost. In the second group we have people who are saved but (carnal) because they have never been challenged to choose the life of intentional discipleship focused on internal transformation. Notice the indictment made by the writer to the Hebrews: *"Though by this time you ought to be teachers"* (Hebrews 5:12 ESV).

Additionally, the second group of "un-discipled" disciples have for lack of a cure, become the normal, and accepted cause of many churches being shut down or on life support! This condition has been accepted by many as a fact of life. It is apparent such churches operate by speculation rather than revelation from the Word, and the Holy Spirit, our Teacher. We will discuss this malady more fully in a later chapter.

Having largely forsaken its mission with God to be a part of kingdom expansion – the church has substituted its own way of doing church as a clubhouse where religious people come together with other people who think, dress, vote, behave, and believe (legalism) like them. Politics have become the new religion ("kid") on the block!

This book is not for you if you are content with this, as the way things are in your church. My goal is to provoke conversations that lead to Spiritual action, risk, rediscovery, and restoration of apostolic, holistic, missional ministry. Many church leaders feel overwhelmed with the challenges of ministry dealing with the present apostasy of youth and young adults and add to the misery, a rising secularly mixed church culture accompanied by an approaching secular worldview. Where do you start [change] in a church culture that prevents it from being mission effective? Do you know the difference between fads and major changes? What will really make a difference in the long haul?

Now, please don't hear what I am not saying! Please let me be clear, the death of the church culture as we have known it will *in no way* be the death of the church. The Church Jesus founded is alive and well – it is right and will survive, for it is eternal. Praise God! There are some in the local church who have not bowed to Baal! The church culture that we are challenging has been confused with a *mixture of law and grace,* both inside and outside the church. We must choose the life:

> "Christianity has no cost in America. We've made it
> way too easy to be "born again" – perhaps much easier
> than Jesus intended. When do we get to the point
> at which we accept smaller numbers of intensely

devoted people rather than feverishly investing in filling
auditoriums and stadiums with massive numbers of
the lukewarm "Christians" that Jesus promised to
spew from his mouth"?[5]

— George Barna

In reality, it is an expression of religion that is in part civil religion where politics, worldview, and lifestyle match; and it is part club where religious people hang out. I do not believe Jesus is pleased that the impact of His great sacrifice on the Cross would be reduced to an invitation for people to join and to support an institution or culture club. The cost to the body of Christ has been huge:

- No longer a vibrant and committed church
- Full of un-discipled disciples
- Open denial of the great Commandment
- Omitting the Great Commission as antiquated
- Flagrant disobedience of Christ's commands
- There is less joy, passion, and fruitfulness
- Lives are wasted
- Life-changing experiences are left untouched
- Churches are accepting this condition as (normal) reality

This is the result of superficial religion: the constant attempt to do outward things *apart* from *inward transformation*. One writer put it this way:

> You … seek to be godly by submitting yourself to
> external rules and regulations and by conforming

---

[5] George Barna, "Barna'3 Beefs #5," in *The State of the Church 2002* (Ventura, Calif, Barna Research Group, 2002), in Bill Hull's, "Choose the Life, (Baker Books, Grand Rapids, MI, 2004) 43

to behavior patterns imposed upon you by the particular Christian society. You have chosen one in which you hope to be found "acceptable." You will in this way perpetuate the pagan habit of practicing religion in the energy *of the flesh,* and in the very pursuit of righteousness commit idolatry in honoring "Christianity more than Christ."[6]

In defiance of God's Word, God's mind, God's will, and God's judgment, men [and women] everywhere are prepared to dedicate to God what God condemns – the energy *of the flesh!* There is nothing quite so nauseating or pathetic as the flesh trying to be holy![7]

Non-Discipleship Christianity

It has been said, "Non-discipleship Christianity" is the elephant in the room; however, we just ignore and deny that it exists; while throwing an extra-large blanket over it. Yet, we feed that rascal resulting in the people:

- Having a low view of salvation.
- Having a low level of commitment.
- Everyone deserves the same investment of time and resources.
- Constantly striving to meet the demands of the immature.
- God's commands are reduced to a question.
- Meeting the demands of the passive aggressive underachievers.
- Keeping the leaders busy arbitrating conflict among who would be leaders.

---

[6] W. Ian Thomas, *The Saving Life of Christ, and the Mystery of Godliness* (Grand Rapids: Zondervan, 1988), 181.

[7] Ibid. 101, 85.

- Due to all of the busyness, the people are not expected to do kingdom work.
- The presence of the unholy trinity (the world, the flesh, and the devil) is considered normal.
- No time for disciple-making – there is just no time left?

A possible Church Model

The focus of this model concerns a collection of people (perhaps you are in this group), who deeply desire to know God – but their stories do not necessarily fit into the "before, now, and after" narrative. That said, "it is wrong to say transformation *is not* happening in their lives."

- Recovery and restoration are less about the destination in this life and all about recognizing and embracing the journey (throughout life).
- The goal of perfection (transformation) will not be complete until we see Jesus! But we must continue to live in God's acceptance (His will, His Word, His way, and His Presence). God's will for our lives is Christlikeness.
- We must celebrate each day of the journey – even the day of failure and struggle.
- Recovery (restoration) ministries strive to create an atmosphere in which "shame" is not welcome! *"For the Son of Man came to seek and to save what was lost"* (Luke 19:10 NIV).

The Church cultural shift

Before the Covid-19 epidemic, people were leaving the church not because we had asked too much of them – but because we definitely had not asked enough of them. Many of them claim to have left because they wanted to maintain their spirituality. Others expressed that their local church (traditions) were doing their families more harm than good. As the churches begin to emerge from the epidemic, I believe it is time for each local church to ask some serious questions about their shared failures in the mission of "making discipleships" [God's will for our lives] – and get it right to the glory of God!

When we give ourselves to the Lord, we heartily commit a willingness to comply with His instructions and demands (see Matthew 11:29). Paul denotes these demands in the commitment (see Romans 12:1):

1. What is the nature of it? We are to present our *whole* body, or self to God – by a heart decision and by sealing the decision with prayer (see Isaiah 6:8). and obedience (see Luke 6:46). Emphasis mine.

2. What are the qualities of it? It is like offering a sacrifice to God – the act of giving Him something that is costly to us (see 2 Samuel 24:24). It is to give our self – our most valued possession.

The apostle described this offering as being:

a. *A living sacrifice* – at salvation, we *died* to our former master, sin and were made alive unto God and to our Lord, Jesus Christ, our new Master (see Galatians 2:20; Romans 6:2-4). We must accept this truth and be responsive to God as we were to sin; the world, the flesh, and the devil (the unholy trinity).

b. *A holy sacrifice* – By this commitment, we set ourselves apart from sin unto God and express our purpose to be God's instrument of righteousness rather than a tool of the devil for his evil works (see Romans 6:12-13; 2 Timothy 2:19-21).

c. *An acceptable sacrifice* – This commitment is pleasing to God (see 2 Corinthians 5:9-10; 1 John 3:22). It allows Him to energize, direct, and use us to do His will and, by this, to glorify Himself (see Luke 6:45; Matthew 5:16; Ephesians 2:8-10).

This commitment is for the purpose of serving God. It is imperative that we all know that it is *impossible* to serve the Lord without the commitment. Without commitment one continues to serve the former evil spiritual matters. This daily commitment allows God to bless us and use us as blessings to others. Have you truly given your heart and life to Christ? Whatever occupies your heart controls your life (see Luke 6:45; Ephesians 3:17). Remember, the Lord will take command only by invitation − however, the devil takes over at every opportunity without invitation.

The local Church is the visible and situated (place), adopted family of God (people), that is being equipped for mission and Christlikeness (purpose), through the indwelling and empowering ministry of the Holy Spirit (presence).[8]

By Grace

The ageless definition of grace is simply God's *"unmerited favor toward man."*

However, when we read the account of Jesus' sufferings as foretold by the prophets and in the Psalms and fulfilled in the Gospels, we realize that we give an extremely limited definition of grace. Quoting from (Titus 3:4, 5 ESV) we can define grace as *"the kindness and love of God our Savior appeared, He saved us not because of works done by us in righteousness."*

---

[8] J.T. English, *Deep Discipleship* (Published by B&H Publishing Group Nashville, TN 2020) 72

"For the law was given through Moses; grace and truth came through Jesus Christ" (John 1:17 ESV). Under the Law of Moses, God *demanded* righteousness from man; but under grace – God *gives* righteousness to man. Please know, we do not have within ourselves the ability *to live sanctified lives* (see Romans 7:18), therefore, Christ **is** our *sanctification.* How do we reach the goal that God has set for us? For one thing, we must be honest with ourselves and admit where we are: as Paul declared. *"Not that I have already attained"* (v. 12). Then, we keep our eyes of faith on Christ and forget the past – past sins and failures also past successes. We must press on *in His power.* The Christian life is not a game, but a race that demands the very best that is in us: *"This one thing I do"* (v.13). Too many Christians live divided lives:

- One part enjoys the things of the world, and the other part tries to live for the Lord. They get ambitious for "things" and begin minding earthly ambitions.
- Our calling is a "high calling" and a "heavenly calling;" and if we live for this world – we lose the prize that goes with our high calling.

The unregenerated person is by nature a child of wrath, a child of the devil (see Eph. 2;2-3); but Christ *is* our redemption. Think about it, Jesus left the Father's bosom and came into this world in a body of flesh. And through His life, death, and resurrection He accomplished the following:

- He bruised the serpent's head (Genesis 3:15).
- He overcame the world (John 16:33).
- He destroyed the works of the devil (1 John 3:8).
- He removed the fear of death (Hebrews 2:9-15).
- He spoiled principalities and powers (Col. 2:15).
- He now holds the keys of hell and of death (Rev. 1:18).

Praise God! Is it any wonder that God blesses us with "all spiritual blessings" in Christ Jesus?

All Spiritual blessings

In this section, I want us to study the "all things" that are ours in Christ by grace. God delights in the unsaved person made a saint by grace through faith in Jesus, the Son. Therefore …. "All are yours, and you are Christ's, and Christ is God's" (1 Corinthians 3:21-23 ESV). Thus, set forth here is the totality of God's bestowment in Christ Jesus.

All spiritual blessings are found in the Lord Jesus Christ. The gospel believer is in Christ and **complete** *"in Him"* (Col. 2:10 NKJV). The only person who ever completely pleased God was His Son, the man Jesus – and the only way you and I can please God is through His Son!

All Wisdom

> *"In Him we have redemption through His blood, the forgiveness of our trespasses, according to the riches of His grace, which He lavished upon us, in all wisdom and insight"* (Ephesians 1:7, 8 ESV).

All wisdom is revealed in the giving of God's love "according to the riches of His grace." The wisdom of man is foolishness to God. In spite of the fact that humans in their thinking have tried to bypass God – but no individual can have rest in his or her mind or peace in their heart until they are in right relationship with God – and no one can be in a right relationship with God until he or she knows God's Son as their personal Savior!

The fear of the Lord is the beginning of knowledge" (Proverbs 1:7 NIV). When we are born again, we fear God, and as a result of godly fear we receive His Son as our personal Savior, Christ is then *made unto us wisdom* – thus we have the mind of Christ and the wisdom of God abiding within us. All the wisdom of the Godhead is wrapped up in our Savior, Jesus Christ:

- We are saved by His amazing grace (see Ephesians 2:8).
- We are led by His precious Spirit (see Romans 8:14).
- We are sealed by His Spirit until the day of redemption (see Ephesians 4:30).
- We are kept by His Power (see Romans 8:38, 39; 1 Peter 1:5).

All that I need I find in Jesus, and I am willing to follow as He leads. I am willing for Him to choose for me, and I am trusting all the days of my future into His hands. I can say with the Psalmist, *"Surely goodness and mercy shall follow me all the days of my life: and I will dwell in the house of the Lord forever"* (Psalm 23:6 NKJV).

All things in Christ

The apostle Paul, God's apostle to the Church, speaks freely of the *"unsearchable riches of Christ"* (Ephesians 3:8 ESV). The riches of His *"kindness* and *forbearance* and *patience"* (Romans 2:4 ESV) and tells us, that God grants *"the forgiveness of our trespasses* according to the riches of *"His grace"* (Ephesians 1:7 ESV). And "My God shall supply every *need of yours according to His riches in glory in Christ Jesus"* (Philippians 4:19 ESV). Emphasis is mine.

Paul is reminded of the relationship between himself and the Philippians with both parties actively involved in the sharing of both material and spiritual gifts. The Philippians are blessed because of the offering they sent to Paul, Paul in turn assures them that the spiritual meaning of their gifts is far more important to him than the gifts themselves. Their joy will be full because of the gifts God will give them. Out of His abundant wealth, God will more than amply take care of the Philippians – and us.

Certainly, during this COVID-19 epidemic and the variants, individually and corporately we have ample opportunities to show our love for Christ and others as we give of our resources and services. What a blessing it is to know that our gifts are looked upon as spiritual sacrifices to the Lord – that rejoices His heart! Paul believed that God was in control no matter what it looked like. No matter the events or circumstances God was able to meet every need (see Romans 8:28).

In times like these, it is refreshing to know that when the child of God is in the will of God, all the universe works for him or her; but when the child of God is out of the will of God – actually, nothing works for them! This is the providence of God.

We can never fully understand the *grace of God* nor the scope of His love for a sinful world. But it is my prayer that through reading this book, Christians may know the riches we possess in Christ – and that unbelievers may come to see the beauty and worth of surrendering their all to Him. This is our prayer for restoration. With that same assurance, we enter a new era, a new season of opportunity.

STUDY GUIDE: CHAPTER 1 IN PURSUIT OF TRUE RESTORATION

1. Jesus commissioned the local churches specifically, to _____ , _____, form, and holistically develop "spiritually mature _____" of Christ (disciples).

2. The local church is not only to equip the saints for ministry but to _____ _____ then in growing in their faith and knowledge of the _____ ____ _____ "to the stature of the _____ __ Christ" (see Ephesian 4:13 ESV).

3. The local church is seriously handicapped by the _____ that the _____ of _____ is _____ rather than _____.

4. The goal of perfection (sanctification) will not be _____ until we see Jesus.

5. A living sacrifice at salvation to our _____ _____ , Satan and were made _____ unto God and our Lord, Jesus Christ our _____ _____.

6. A holy sacrifice, by this commitment, we set ourselves _____ _____ ____ unto God and express our purpose to be God's _____.

7. Certainly during this epidemic and its variants, God is still in control, no matter what it may look like. No matter the _____ or circumstances God is able to meet _____ _____.

CHAPTER TWO

LIFE IN THE SPIRIT

"For those who live according to the flesh set their minds on the things of the flesh, but those who live according to the Spirit set their minds on the things of the Spirit. For to set the mind on the flesh is death, but to set the mind on the Spirit is life and peace" (Romans 8:5-6 ESV).

Today it is crucial that the body of Christ strive to know and experience all we can of the "life and walk" in the Spirit. Numerous Christian leaders and other influencers have built massive ministry platforms over the years. Their pageantry and numerical success cannot be denied. However, much of it is offered as what they are willing to offer God even on the brink of losing what God really requires of them. We see and hear from all corners, that in order to be acceptable today Christianity must undergo a make-over to make it an inclusive and palatable *religion* – even to affirm the salvation of people of other religions. Much of this false teaching is presented under the banner of love and compassion.

Many particularly influential people drop big-money for the cheers, affirmation, and support of their progressive-secular agenda. In the process, of course, the hard truths of Christianity are tweaked, omitted, redefined, or just ignored. Legalism and religion always appeal to the flesh, teaching to control people through behavior modification, which make those pastors who yield to this model, mere sin managers.

In such churches progressive sanctification is practiced but never expected to be attained in the Christian's earthly lifetime. Legalists and religionists do not trust in the *finished* work of Christ and the efficacy of His blood to produce His intended result. The apostle Paul came *against this lie* and addressed the problem in Galatians 3:1-3:

> "O foolish Galatians! Who has bewitched you? It was before your eyes that Jesus Christ was publicly portrayed is crucified. Let me ask you only this. Did you receive the Spirit by works of the law or by hearing with faith? Are you so foolish? Having begun in the Spirit, are you now being perfected by the flesh?" ESV.

Paul calls the Galatians Christians foolish! How could they believe one is perfected in a manner other than the way one is saved and justified? They were saved; they received the Spirit by hearing with faith and they are perfected, sanctified, in the same manner. The flesh can never produce the level of perfection God requires to be in union with Him.

Pure Mockery

Sadly to many people, the church in America is an outdated non-essential failure. On one of the morning TV shows in June 2021. I could hardly believe what I was seeing. One of the hosts performing a live wedding ceremony. The bride and groom appeared before him with their own vows, which each read to the other. He then pronounced them husband and wife in the name of the network. It was obvious God had no part in it! All the laughter and gaiety expressed after the ceremony – plainly showed that to them, God and the church were jokes. In mid-July, a transgender bishop from a traditional denomination was the featured guest on this same network morning show.

More concerning to Bible-believing Christians is the fact the media generally opposes our biblical values. These watchkeepers of information are indoctrinating *the public rather than informing them.* The media conditions people to *think less of Christianity* and never favorable even to positive contributions to society. Another concern is the media is censoring, deleting, flagging, and silencing believers without apology. Where have all the shepherds gone? The church is God's counter cultural, if we don't speak out the pertinent truth of God's Word – who will?

The world probably doesn't know the church is back from the COVID-19 closure in fact, for their sakes we better let them know that, even though the church buildings were shut down [many still remain closed], the true spiritual Church of Jesus Christ (the Body of Christ) has never closed (see Revelation 3:7).

True love and compassion

Our churches should be refuge houses for sinners, sanctuaries for the hurt, those who are fearful, confused and do not know where to go, the oppressed, the lonely, and certainly hospitals for the soul. But despite COVID-19, I see much of contemporary church culture *willfully* submitting to the secular culture in many areas of life, especially in areas of sexuality, and non-biblical worldly involvement, rather than giving the gospel first priority no matter what. Many churches across this country strive to make Christianity appealing, by removing or relaxing the biblical anchors (the Holy Trinity, the truth of God's Word, the Christians' walk in the Spirit now, and future judgments). Listen, the secular world is speaking:

- Do not be narrow they chide (broaden your religious horizons)
- Be totally inclusive
- Be more affirming
- Listen to the culture
- Allow culture to conform your thinking
- Let culture raise your children

Sadly, we are no longer committed to *"the whole counsel of God"* (Acts 20:27 ESV). How much of the secular culture are we going to accept in order to redeem it? Throughout the history of the church that question has been widely discussed. What we can and cannot accept are biblically crucial to our Christian witness individually and corporately. What concerns me most is the stuff secular culture is shoving down our throats in the name of love, compassion, and relevance from the bottom of Satan's barrel of most enticing temptations and snares.

Many ultra-liberals and ultra-conservatives in the ranks of Christianity today believe that traditional Christianity has failed them, so they want to make it over, claiming it is out of touch with the culture and the shifting values of society. Much of the church is *willingly* submitting to this deception, while feeling self-righteously good. One of the churches of Asia Minor that John wrote about: The church of Sardis was in a similar position as we find ourselves facing today. Jesus concluded His evaluation of that church with the following message:

"I know your works, you have the reputation of being alive,
but you are dead. Wake up and strengthen what remains and
is about to die, for I have not found your works complete in
the sight of my God" (Revelation 3:1-3 ESV).

No doubt the church at Sardis settled down and gave in to the temptations of the sexually charged secular culture – failing to stand against it. Yet! Praise God, not everyone in the church caved in with the culture. Jesus went on to say,

"Yet you still have a few names in Sardis, people who have
not soiled their garments, and they will walk with me in
white, for they are worthy." (v.4)

Sounds about like the present day in the American Church, unfortunately, many of our local churches have a reputation of spiritual life because of their lively sermons and, music, but the spirits of many Bible-believing men and women are dead (see Rev. 3:1). In this manner, a rising generation exists that really knows "How to have church" without God's presence. Praise God there are at least a few who have not contaminated their garments with the sensuality gone wild populace. We talk so much about revival in the land. Are we really prepared for a flood of newly born again converts to fill our churches? What would they be fed if they visited your church this Sunday morning?

REVIVAL HAPPENS WHEN SOMETHING THAT ONCE LIVED IS BROUGHT TO LIFE!

Revival happens when something once living is brought back to life. Comparable in this situation to the doctor taking shock pads to a lifeless body, causing the heart to begin beating in rhythm again. Here we take the shock pads to the heart of *a lifeless church body*. The time has come when we need to:

- revive the old revival strategies
- restore the standard of holiness
- resurrect the preaching of the entire gospel of Christ
- restore the (backbone of any ministry) with prayer and intercession vigils
- restore biblical standards to leadership

It has been said that "many of our congregations know how to grow without growing the people who sit therein." We have substituted "a strong anointing with "good vibes" to try and soothe the congregation. Many churches never get around to worshipping Jesus at all. Instead, they idolize deeply engrained traditions of men over the presence of the Holy Spirit in services. The presence of the Lord has been expelled from the church because of a shortage of "bold" gospel preaching. To awaken this generation, God can only use those who have been revived in spirit.

The GPS is manmade

My wife and I were on our way to a Sunday morning preaching engagement in Boston, Mass. It was late Friday evening, so we decided to get a hotel room in New

Haven, Conn. and hit the road early Saturday morning to arrive for an afternoon reception. My wife punched in the address to the hotel and away we went following directions from the GPS. Across the city we went, then down some side streets ending up in a large vacant lot surrounded by forest – where the hotel once stood? The GPS said, "You have arrived at your destination." Wow! However, after a little "dead reckoning" we ended up just outside of the main entrance to Yale University. There we were directed to a hotel down the street from the entrance.

We entered the hotel, and I asked the desk clerk about a first-floor room, would you believe she refused and gave us a room on the top floor. I protested and she said, "tell me about in in the morning." The bellhop opened the door and grinned at us – it was a suite with a full kitchen with many goodies, a large full living room and dining area, two bedrooms each had a fabulous bathroom with a jacuzzi. Having just completed a night tour of New Heaven – after driving up from Fayetteville, North Carolina [home]. It was such a great gesture! All we wanted was a shower and bed! [a VIP had cancelled out]. I thought of a book I had read titled "Religious but Lost!" We were making the journey with an inaccurate guidance system. Is your GPS accurate? Only Christ is the correct answer!

With Eternity in View – Get Right or Get Left

In His grand plan of (salvation and reconciliation), God incorporated the perfect spiritual guidance system, consisting of the Holy Spirit, and the Word working in tandem. For various reasons many Christians choose to rely on their natural faculties of the "flesh" for guidance. When Adam fell his spirit sank deep down into his soul, sending the soul deep down into the body, the flesh – "for he is indeed flesh"(Genesis 6:3 NKJV).

These words describe humanity as they are now when unregenerated. Many Christians live defeated lives because they do not know how to live in the Spirit. Perhaps they are not knowledgeable of this spirit-life as it is revealed in the New Testament – the tri-parts of man. The Apostle Paul writes, *"Now may the God of peace himself sanctify you completely, and may your whole spirit, and soul, and body be kept blameless at the coming of our Lord Jesus Christ"* (I Thessalonians 5:23 ESV):

1. Spirit – the inner temple where God the Holy Spirit dwells.
2. Soul – the mental and emotional life, making up the personality.
3. Body – is the outside case, or the shell. Flesh!

Your body is not all of you. Your mind is the faculty for thinking, but your spirit is to be the active power and, it is also in your spirit, that the Holy Spirit dwells. Placed in order of importance by the Apostle Paul, [spirit, soul, and body].

The New Covenant and the Indwelling Holy Spirit

The Body of Christ desperately needs a fresh unveiling of God's New Covenant today. We need it because our generation is living in a day of powerful demonic seductions. Jesus warned of these days in which Satan would attempt to deceive even the very elect of God. Today we are seeing Jesus' words come to pass, as humankind is challenged by an overwhelming flood of temptations never experienced by any past generation.

Without a doubt, the devil has practically taken control of the media. Just a few years ago the airwaves were not polluted, but today the atmosphere is saturated with pornography of all grades beamed to homes the world over. Technological advances has produced gifts for our wellbeing meant to improve our lives, but as the same Satan has opened wide the floodgates of evil; and society is being inundated by seductions that are coming upon us with ferocity we've never seen before.

> Satan is using every form of media to feed dormant lusts, encourage promiscuity and destroy every semblance of morality.

In the process he is breaking up homes, and marriage and the family. Tragically, many Christians are being swept up in the demonic web of sensuality "self-effort." Believers who have linked themselves with secret sins are now battling for their souls. People tell us of life-controlling habits in their own lives and lives of loved ones – habits such as drugs, alcohol, pornography, adultery, fornication, homosexuality, gambling, anger, bitterness, and stealing.

Many of these people sincerely love the Lord. They have prayed, cried, and sought counseling from pastors and friends yet nothing seems to free them. They feel chained, **unable to break free from sin's power.** Many such Christians have concluded they can never be free from their sin. They are afraid they will never **be able to move out of the bondage of flesh,** Paul describes in Romans 7. Paul says, this person does what they hate, **with no power** to do the right thing. He or she is unable to move into the spiritual freedom Paul outlines in Romans 8, **where power over the dominion of sin is revealed.** In the eyes of this bound person, there is no escape from the wretchedness of always doing what he or she **despises.** So, the individual, has resigned him or herself to struggling for the rest of their life. Living from paycheck to paycheck, your overhead is too high. You have so little, but impulsive spending takes that.

God begins His work by regenerating the *spirit* of a person. Then He adds, "And I will put My Spirit within you" (Ezekiel 36:26-27 ESV). Notice, Paul continually refers to his own spirit apart from the Spirit of God. We are born of the Spirit when God regenerates our human spirit, giving us a *new spirit* "[the New Covenant]. That which is born of the Spirit is spirit" (John 3:6 ESV).

As stated earlier, becoming a child of God is not becoming a member of a church and looking like a Christian, Jesus said, *"I tell you a truth, no one can see the kingdom of God unless he is born again"* (John 3:3 NIV). And what agreement has the temple of God with idols? For you are the temple of the living God. As God has said:

> "I will **dwell** in them
> And **walk** among them,
> I will be their God,
> And they shall be My people."
> 2 Corinthians 6:16 NKJV

Paul exclaims, "since we have these **promises**, beloved, let us repent, and cleanse ourselves (through the Word and the Spirit) from every defilement of spirit, soul, and body, bringing holiness to completion in the fear of God" (2 Corinthians 7:1 ESV). Emphasis added throughout. There is a cleansing of the spirit that God may dwell in us. Based on the ground of the precious blood of Jesus Christ – God cleanses us from sin. Please retain this point, because we cannot enter God's presence laden with sin. Remember, as gospel believers we are invited to "come boldly to the throne of grace, that we may obtain mercy and find grace to help in time of need" (Hebrews 4:16 NKJV). Emphasis added.

This command strongly contrasts with God's command at Mt. Sinai: *"Do not go up to the mountain or touch its base"* (see Ex. 19:12 NKJV). Because of Christ's priestly work, gospel believers can approach God's presence. The writer of Hebrews is expressing the openness of God's call *in Christ,* "Come" (see Revelation 22:17). This invitation by the Spirit remains open to anyone who will come by faith in Christ to accept the Lord's gracious offer of eternal Life.

At the Cross

One of my main purposes in writing this book is to emphasize the lack of knowledge and practice of the life and "walk after the Spirit." **First of all, without "this walk" we are dead!** If we are going to live above the increasing satanic flurry of the things of earth and triumph in spiritual warfare – our spirit *must be* liberated so that it can take its rightful place of *spiritual* dominance over the soul and body. Once our spirit has been born again – God and Christ reside in this most holy place [body] through the Holy Spirit and the Word.

Until Adam's fall his spirit was dominant and acted through the soul and body which were subservient to his spirit from creation. Adam was *like* Christ until the fall. At the fall of Adam, his spirit [now dead] fell into his soul; giving the dominant position up to the soul and body, "the flesh," for "he is flesh"(Genesis 6:3 ESV).

Here then is the description of the unregenerated person, "flesh." Adam was created in the image of God, but his sin marred that image, therefore, Adam's sin and marred image were passed on to all his descendants including those of *us* who are alive today. When we are "born again" our spirit was recreated into the image of Christ (2 Cor. 5:17 ESV).

Prayerfully read 2 Corinthians 5:1-21, soak your heart in this truth of God's Word before moving on. Your spiritual life depends on it! Jay Leach

---

"A new creation"

The Apostle Paul put much emphasis on the order of man from God's perspective, spirit, soul, and body. God began His work by regenerating the spirit in man. We are born with a natural human spirit of which God says, "And I will give you a new heart and a new spirit I will put within you. And I will remove the heart of stone from your flesh and give you a heart of flesh. And I will put my Spirit within you and cause you to walk in my statutes and be careful to obey my rules" (Ezekiel 36:26-27 ESV). We will cover this fully in the next chapter.

We are born again of the Holy Spirit when God regenerates the human spirit, giving us a new spirit. "That which is born of the Spirit is spirit" (John 3:6 ESV). How does God work this out? It is at Calvary where God does the work in us. The Scripture said of our Lord and Savior:

> *"For Christ also suffered once for sins, the righteous for the unrighteous, that He might bring us to God, **being put to death in the flesh but made alive in the spirit**"* (1 Peter 3:18 ESV) Emphasis mine.

As you enter the fellowship of Christ's death your spirit is quickened (made alive) and brought into resurrection union with Him in newness of life (see Romans 6:1-10). It is imperative that we understand that – "knowing the cross is the very basis for this life in the Spirit." So, just as Christ was put to death on the cross, and quickened in the spirit, so must each of us "be put to death in the flesh." The flesh must be crucified (see Galatians 5:24) so that as believers we "walk by the Spirit" daily, and do not fulfill the lusts of the flesh.

Saint or Sinner not both

In this section we will get down to the nitty gritty. If you are a sinner, you have not been saved by grace. If you have been saved by grace, you are not a sinner. If you have been "saved by grace," rather than saying "I'm a sinner saved by grace." Then you were once a sinner, but now you are completely something else! Paul addresses Christians as *"saints"* in many of his letters, and never uses the term *"sinner"* to identify believers. Remember! We are talking about a *"state of being,"* not an "act" or "action" when we use the term "sinner." We were born with a sin nature — and that <u>is precisely why we had to be born again!</u> Thus, my new nature is not a sin nature – but a sinless nature. I can sin but I am not a sinner. We are either *(in Adam with a sin nature)* or *(in Christ with a sinless nature).* That is a true fact folks, there are no other categories! *A state of being: Either a saint or sinner:*

1. A saint can sin, but that sin <u>does not undo the work that Christ did to make him or her a saint.</u>
2. A sinner can do good works, <u>but good works do not make a sinner a saint.</u>

Two schools of thought

Two of the main Reformers Luther and Calvin agreed on the approach that says:

- One is saved by grace through faith, <u>but then for the rest of his or her earthly life they must *try their best to modify their behavior to please God and release blessing in our lives*</u> be right with God or pleasing to Him depends on their behavior – do my best to keep the rules here and hang on until I get to heaven. I will be fully sanctified then (legalism).

Many of the rules are not even closely related to Scripture – which is the usual way *legalism* works. Almost all Protestant churches, no matter the denomination, when all is said and done, soon you will hear *a mixture of law and grace.* The idea that we can trust Christ with no intention of *obeying* Him is an illusion generated by an unbelieving church culture. Some have grasped another lie of the culture, that we can trust Christ for salvation, but following Him is optional. Upon a visit to the United States the late Mahatma Gandhi of India is reported to have said, "If Christians would live according to their beliefs, all people would become Christians."

In other words, we are living according to *our beliefs,* and what it proves is that *we do not believe Jesus.* The sad result of this is local churches and individuals therein living lives full of religious activity without transformation (discipleship). Pastors are we shepherds, or have we become mere sin managers?

Like the sons of Issachar, "we must be aware of the times." *"Men who had understanding of the times, to know what Israel ought to do"* (1 Chron. 12:32 ESV).

Christ (alone) is Lord and King over His Church

Christians are experiencing increasing amounts of bias and even persecution for their beliefs. This is not happening just here in America, but around the world. Governments, powerful corporations, and many of our foundational institutions are working together to *censor the role of Christianity in public life.* This includes leaders of the *culture,* not just smaller political leaders – but leaders of academia, the media, the marketplace, economics, sports, and I am sad to say, the military. All of these *leaders of the culture* will come together, not 100%, but enough.

We are familiar with this type of coalition at work over the past five decades their goal and schemes are to *drive the influence of the Word of God out of the culture!"* It was recently reported on the news, that 70% of our leading scientists are atheists. Remember, the Bible prophecies about the increase in knowledge during the last days. We used to wonder why more knowledge would be so bad for us – certainly we do not have to wonder any longer.

Look at our universities and the scientific community, we see that the most educated and intelligent people on the planet are some of the most wicked, worldly, and ignorant about spiritual things. This can be the most exciting time realizing that Christ is soon to return, or it can be the most nerve-racking time knowing that final judgment is also coming. Satan and his demons are well aware of this, so they are rushing the world toward the fulfillment of end-time prophecies described in the Books of Daniel and Revelation. Are you ready for this?

Worldly voices began to speak loudly about a one world government and how one super leader could manage and make resources available quicker for aiding the whole world. I'm sure that some of the atheistic leaders want to test this idea during the coronavirus epidemic. And certainly, we do not know where COVID-19 and the "variants" will take this nation or any other nation of the world, but one thing is sure – all nations are affected by it.

As America and the world become more secular-minded, we can expect more and more attacks on the people and the things of God. The post-quarantine era may prove to be one of the most challenging seasons churches and their leaders. These worldly voices will grow louder and louder! One world government and the seven-year tribulation are approaching faster than we can imagine. Somethings we have heard about through the news, and yet many things have changed due to COVID-19 that we do not know about yet, but one thing we do know – many things some good and some bad have changed forever.

In the Scriptures, we have seen how voluntary disobedience has caused nations and great people to fall. Earlier, we saw that voluntary disobedience caused the Fall of Adam and Eve and then there was Israel's first king, Saul, who lost his kingdom because of his *voluntary* disobedience.[9] We must stand in the Lord's holy presence by the power of the Holy Spirit.

Political agendas versus Obeying the Word of God

To secular society's mindset, God's Word binds and stifles their human potential.

The coronavirus presented ample opportunity for the secularists and atheists to make their move:

1. Lock the church doors because they are non-essential. We got this!
2. Put the community on lock-down, that weakens and limits their reach and power of Christianity during the pandemic.
3. Thus, the atheistic scientists' cry became, "we will only deal with science and facts."
4. Therefore, the church is deemed non-essential. Meaning [God and Christianity are no longer needed]? Again, I repeat the recorded statistic 70% of America's top scientists are atheists.

In Revelation 3:8, Jesus told the pastor of the Church of Philadelphia, *"I have set before you an open door, that no one can shut."* Though these words were written to a specific local Church in Asia Minor, they have echoed for 2000 years throughout the New Testament era, reminding every church that Christ is King and Lord over the church, He alone has authority over the church. Again, Jesus told the angel of the church in Philadelphia ".... I know your works" Revelation 3:7a-8a).

As I mentioned in an earlier section, in recent years, it seems that much of the Church in America has become confused about its beginning, and its prophetic place in God's great plan. This has led many people to question the value and relevancy of the church today.

---

[9] Jay Leach, *The Apostolic Rising* (Trafford Publishing 2021) 48

"What purpose does the church serve?" More harmful is the reality that more and more people today are comfortable with not attending church at all.

Additionally, thousands who attended church prior to the COVID-19 have now found it much more comfortable and convenient to stay at home. Then many have decided to wait and see. Have we forgotten our mandate in Hebrews 10:25? Based on the Scripture, it became evident that though God did not cause the COVID-19 pandemic, I believe, He is using it to *test* His church and *purify* His people.

Sadly, COVID-19 has become a standoff between politics and obedience to the Word of God. The clash of societal issues will demand first place, trumping a biblical worldview. As we continue moving through 2021, I believe the church will be *tested* again perhaps it will be through *persecution?* The church *always* refines its convictions during persecutions. Especially during these trying times, I believe people are looking for something that transcends the *circumstances of their life,* of the culture, and even of what is going on in our nation. Especially today when it is a challenge for the world to get up in the morning to face all of the uncertainties.

The church must come to their rescue because we have Jesus. Our Lord said we Christians are the light of the world and must be as a light set on a hill, not hiding at home. Notice, in Revelation 2, Jesus commended the church in Ephesus for their faith and perseverance under hard circumstances. Then He continued in saying what should be a *warning* for us today:

> "But I have this against you, that you have abandoned the love you had at first. Remember therefore from where you have fallen; and repent and do the works you did at first. If not, I will come to you and remove your lampstand from its place, unless you repent" (Revelation 2:4-5 ESV).

A lampstand means influence and place in society. We do know looking back at Church history, the lampstand at Ephesus was removed. We must make sure that we are doing kingdom work as commanded by or Lord. "Making disciples!" The true church has got to be visible! Jesus is also the only hope for sinners to be saved and gain eternal life. People are concerned about their bodies and physical health. The church must remind them that their most important need is a blood-washed spiritual life and health.

Therefore, repent, church! We must return to bold allegiance to God. If the world does not appreciate the value of Christianity part of the blame falls on us. It is time to wake up and recognize the evil secular and, atheistic agendas are advancing and plotting their next move. Other world powers in the past centuries have stood where America stands today and cannot be found. Why? Because they turned their backs on God. Many dangerous people are obtaining very high positions with a goal to destroy America and recast it in their own image.

Every aspect of our society keeps moving further away from biblical principles, but God is not mocked, neither has God's Word changed. As more and more political pressure come against believers – the Lord will probably use these things as a discipline to refine the true church.

Though we believe the saints will rapture before the onslaught of Armageddon, the church must return to its purpose "The Great Commission" and Christians being conduits for the Holy Spirit to work through in preparing the people for the present-day, stepped-up activities of Satan and his demons, *"because he knows he has but a short time"* (Revelation 12:12 NKJV).

A holy people

As blood-washed believers, we are to be brought into ever-deepening fellowship with Christ's death. The sword (Word of God) must be thrust deeper and deeper into our earthly life. The Holy Spirit must be allowed to apply the death of Christ's cross to you and let the Word of God cut, piercing to the division of the soul and spirit.

Rather than the post-pandemic church going back to the same old mundane of numbers and building sizes? Perhaps, it would be more feasible to move from numbers and wider to narrow and deeper! Jay Leach

---

Until God cuts deeper and deeper none of us know just how intimately connected, we are to this present evil world and the things thereof. All self-trust must be put to death, and again we have to be brought to a point beyond our power to endure – where we are compelled to trust in the God who raises the dead (study carefully 2 Corinthians 1:8-9; 13:2). You will find the same truth in Romans 7:4, *"Likewise, my brothers, you also have died to the law through the body of Christ, so that you may belong to another, to Him who has been raised from the dead, in order that we may bear fruit for God"* (ESV).

"Being put to death in the flesh" – is not a one-time operation, but an ongoing matter. As I stated earlier, the Word of God is the instrument God uses through the Holy Spirit for this deep separation of the soul and spirit (see 1 Thess. 5:23). You can discern the difference between that which comes into your mind, the intellect, and what is of God in your spirit, if not, simply ask Him to teach you, for the Holy Spirit is the Teacher.

Again, this separation is essential so that your "born again" spirit may act in purity, without the input of a mixture from those of the soulish life. Their (minds) are *darkened in their understanding,* (Eph. 4:18 ESV), the god of this world hath *blinded the mind* (2 Cor. 4:4 KJV), which is only renewed, and the veil destroyed, up to the extent that the *light of truth* penetrates the mind – whatever the person is able to apprehend. Just because we have left the club scene doesn't mean the club has left us. How do we know the difference? Only by experiencing the truth of God's Word and by God letting it work in you to the dividing of soul and spirit.

It is clear that we have many mental concepts of God's Word and truth which never came from the Holy Spirit. If we want our churches to live, we must make every effort to ensure we protect and proclaim the true gospel of Jesus Christ.

The gospel is our life!

One of the greatest hindrances to the gospel and the Holy Spirit revealing to us "the will of God" is our mental concepts from speculation. Even though we already know that the Word of God is God's will. We will discuss this hindrance further in the next chapter. The writer of Hebrews says,

> "For the Word of God is living and active, sharper than any two-edged sword, piercing to the division of soul and spirit, of joints and of marrow, and discerning the thoughts and intentions of the heart" (Hebrews 4:12 ESV).

The Word of God is not only a sword, but also a mirror that brings us into the very presence of the Holy God who desires truth in the inward parts. The Christian who abides in the Word is judged, chastened, connected, led, and rebuked. Such a believer cries out with David,

> "Search me, O God, and know my heart: try me, and know my thoughts: and see if there be any wicked way in me and lead me in the way everlasting" (Psalm 139: 23, 24 KJV).

This is a Christian who finds peace which passes all understanding, and without the conviction, chastening, and correction that comes through diligent and untiring study of the Word there can be no complete peace and rest in Christ Jesus. Very few Christians enjoy their spiritual birthright because they do not study diligently to show themselves approved unto God – looking into the mirror of the perfect law of liberty, the Word of the living God. Jesus came from heaven to earth to declare the Father (see John 1:18):

- He had unshakable faith in God.
- His love was inexhaustible and unchanging.
- He gave all expecting nothing in return.
- He was just, but He died for the unjust.
- He was sinless, yet He was made sin for us that we might be made the righteousness of God in Him.
- He lived, loved, and died for us – and if we hear His Word and believe His Word, it brings eternal life to our hearts. Give Him praise and glory!

Just as God looked into the hearts of the people in Noah's day and saw the wickedness of humanity, He declared that He would destroy man from the earth (see Genesis 6:5). Please continue reading! God has not changed, nor is He blinking at sin. He cannot be deceived. He is omniscient. He hears all and He sees all!

When we play the hypocrite and get by with it before men, we are playing the fool before a Holy God! Jay Leach

---

Those persons who refuse to hear the Word will be judged by the very Word they refuse to hear! Jesus said, *"The one who rejects Me and does not receive My words has a judge; the word that I have spoken will judge him on the last day"* (John 12:48 ESV).

It is comforting to know that our great High Priest can be touched with a feeling of our infirmities and weaknesses. He knows, He understands, He cares, He sees and is able to supply our every need. As our brother in the flesh, He is experienced in our infirmities and temptations. As the only begotten Son of God who became the Son of man, He is victorious, and as God He acts on our behalf.

He is now seated, *the Man, Jesus is* in glory – our Savior, our Mediator, our Intercessor, and our Advocate. Remember! Jesus is not seated on a throne of judgment, but on the throne of grace!

We have sinned and therefore we do not deserve *mercy;* but because He bore our sins and paid our penalty, when we have faith in His finished work, we receive *mercy in time of need.* When our faith is in His shed blood, we are accepted in the Beloved. Praise God!

STUDY GUIDE: CHAPTER 2 LIFE IN HE SPIRIT

1. It is crucial that the body of Christ strive to _____ and _____ all we can of the "life and walk" in the Spirit.

2. Legalism and _____ always appeal to the flesh, teaching to control people through _____ _____, which make those pastors who yield to this model, mere sin managers.

3. No doubt the church at Sardis settled down and gave in to the _____ of the sexually charged _____ _____.

4. The Spirit life as revealed in the New Testament as the _____ of man.

5. So, just as Christ was _____ to _____ on the cross and quickened in the _____, so must each of us be put to death in the flesh.

6. It is comforting to know that our great High Priest can be touched with a feeling of our _____ and _____.

7. Just as Christ was put to death on the cross, and quickened in the spirit, so must each of us, "be put to death in the _____."

CHAPTER THREE

"My covenant I will not break, nor altar the word that has gone out of my lips" (Psalm 89:34).

In this chapter, I want to show you the need for the indwelling power of the Holy Spirit. I want to emphasize from the start that no one *in his or her own strength* is able to live an overcoming life, free from sin's power and dominion. A person may grieve over committed sins, shedding continuous tears, but in his or her own willpower and ability cannot defeat powerful besetting sins.

When the prophet Ezekiel preached *repentance* to the nation of Israel, he knew that God was grieved over Israel's backsliding and compromise. He told the people:

> *"Repent and turn from all your transgressions, lest iniquity be your ruin. Cast away from you all the transgressions that you have committed and make yourselves a **new heart and a new spirit!** Why will you die, O house of Israel? For I have no*

40

pleasure in the death of anyone, declares the Lord GOD, so turn and live" (Ezekiel 18:30-32 ESV). Emphasis added throughout.

In essence, Ezekiel was telling them, "You know what you are doing is wrong, so why don't you stop it? Put it down. Turn from it, make a change in yourself. Get yourself a new heart." Ezekiel himself enjoyed the overcoming power of the Holy Spirit in his own life. He was one of a number of Old Testament prophets whose holy lives were due solely to *the indwelling Holy Spirit*. The Spirit Himself gave them the needed inner resources to overcome temptation and sin. Though the Spirit had not been poured out yet; God in His mercy gave His Spirit to those who were called to do some great work. And so it was with Ezekiel who testified, ***"And as He spoke to me the Spirit entered into me"*** (Ezekiel 2:2 ESV).

But Ezekiel's audience had no idea of their need for the indwelling presence of God's Spirit. They could not overcome their sin no matter how hard they tried. This same problem is very prevalent in the church today. Like Ezekiel, many pastors are baffled that the people do not become convicted by God's Word, heed His powerful warnings, and turn themselves around. That's why he urged them, "You need to motivate yourselves to turn away from sin. You need to get yourself a new spirit." I preached this same Old Covenant message for years, "Why are you letting yourself go? Your sins are ruining you?" At the same time I was experiencing sin that I so dearly wanted to bring out of others. A way out of Romans 7! No matter how many sins I commit, it is always the one sin-principle working in me that leads to them. I need forgiveness for my sins, but I need deliverance from the *power* of sin. The former touches my conscience, the latter touches my life. One day, I realized that I was dying as a result of this secret sinful weakness in my own life. I repented and this time I moved over into

Romans 8, praise God! I definitely want people to repent and turn from their wickedness.

Though saved early in life and leaving home at 18 years of age, I didn't give my local church time to disciple me. Such preaching has its purpose, because it makes people *realize their inability* to stop sinning in their own power – and produces in them a *crisis* that drives them to the cross. The Holy Spirit holding up God's Word as a mirror before us reveals the enormous sinfulness of sin.

Just do it?

Just do it! The problem with that was, asking people to do something that is totally impossible in their *own* strength. I have many books in my library on the subject of holiness and sanctification; and they are convicting and saying the same thing! "God demands holiness, purity, and obedience." They also warn us of the consequences of continuing in sin, clearly defines the commands of Christ. These books essentially say, "Here is what is demanded of you. And here is what will happen to you if you don't get it together."

Like many of our local churches, much writing today does not tell us how to obtain the power and authority to obey. I had read many of these books through the years without understanding God's New Covenant provisions. The message to "just do it" is impossible. It was just as impossible in Ezekiel's day. The children of Israel had none of the power they needed to **turn themselves** from sin and cast off their iniquity.

They could no more create in themselves a new heart than they could raise a dead sheep. This was the main problem of the Old Covenant, it demanded perfect obedience, and complete turning from sin – but the command was not accompanied by the indwelling power of the Holy Spirit to obey. This is why God made a New Covenant with humanity.

None but the righteous

Surely, there were believers in Israel who heard Ezekiel's message and hungered for righteousness. There was a holy remnant in Israel at that time. I believe that when they heard Ezekiel's powerful and convicting message, they shouted, "That's what I want a new heart; and be free from sin and shame. But I keep on failing! I've done all that's *humanly possible* to do! I suffered this sinful malady for years until my wife and I became a part of a Spirit-filled church that taught and lived their lives in the Spirit. Praise God! As I pointed out, under the New Covenant God demands total obedience of His people. God commands us to turn aside from all our iniquities – are you listening?

Ezekiel had to be totally upset over what he saw going on in Israel. God's people were scattered, and the priests were busy with their own welfare, pulling in all the wealth for themselves. They cheated the people living off the fat of the offerings while the people suffered. People wandered everywhere *looking for spiritual food, with no shepherds to feed them, lead them, or bind up their wounds.* The Scripture says, the Israelites were still living in sin and trusting in their own righteousness. God told Ezekiel, *"They hear your words, but they do not do them; for with the mouth they show much love, but their hearts pursue ... their own gain ... They hear your words, but they do not do them"* (Ezekiel 33:31–32).

The Source of Power

In this dark hour, God shared a great mystery. He was about to lift Ezekiel out of the Old Covenant surroundings and reveal to him a glorious work that would take place in the time of the Messiah. God was about to unveil the New Covenant for him. Suddenly, Ezekiel's mouth was filled with the Word of the Lord. Ezekiel began preaching a message – God spoke *through* him:

"I will sprinkle clean water on you, and you shall be clean from all your uncleanness, and from all your idols I will cleanse you. And I will give you a new heart, and a new spirit I will put within you. And I will remove the heart of stone from your flesh and give you a heart of flesh. And <u>I will put my Spirit within you, and cause you to walk in my statutes and be careful to obey my rules</u>" (Ezekiel 36:25-27 ESV).

This message was almost too good to be true, God was saying, "I am going to put My Spirit in sin-bound people, and My Spirit will cause them to fulfill every command I have ever gave them. They have come to the end of themselves, Ezekiel. They are dead to any ability to overcome. **But My Spirit is going to empower them to turn away from their sin.**" "Praise God!" I've been telling them to clean themselves up and get a new heart. But now You are saying the day is coming when You will do it for them, by your Spirit! I bid you, in fact I'm pleading with you to hear what the Spirit is saying. Every newscast echoes this need as changes since the beginning of the coronavirus epidemic have been thrown at us so fast that people are not able to process them. Across America, it seems that every age group has been affected mentally. The prince of this world (the devil) has really stepped up his game, knowing his time is short. Notice, God put His Spirit into the new spirit *in* Ezekiel (see Ezekiel 33:31-32), the conditions of the people Ezekiel faced are very prevalent in our Christian communities today. The Scripture says,

"But are not in the flesh but in the Spirit, if indeed the Spirt of God dwells in you. Now if anyone who does not have the Spirit of Christ, he is not His. And if Christ is in you, the body Is dead because of sin, but the Spirit is life because of righteousness" (Romans 8:9-10 NKJV).

In spite of what God's Word has spoken in the text above, many people still believe there are ways around it. Christians no longer live according to the flesh, under control of their sinful human nature. Instead, as stated earlier, with the Spirit living in them, teaching and empowering them – they can live in a way pleasing to God. I pray now that you see the catastrophic condition in us without Him!

The missing link

I'm sure we agree that the missing link in most of our churches is the Holy Spirit along with His gifts and ministries. One of the best ways to activate people in the gifts of the Spirit is to teach them the flows of the Spirit. Jesus taught His disciples that the Holy Spirit would flow out of their innermost being (see John 7:37-39):

- He described the Work of the Spirit in salvation as *"streams of living water will flow from within him"* (John 7:37 NIV).
- In John 4 above, Jesus describes another dimension of being filled with the Spirit as *"rivers of living water"* flowing out of us.
- A companion passage to the verse in Ezekiel 49:9 likened to water flowing from high elevations to lower.
- The Holy Spirit was sent from Heaven flowing into the earth – seeking out the low places of human suffering, weakness, and bondage.
- He seeks out those who are lost, hurting, and living in darkness.
- Each of us in Christ are seated together with Him in heavenly places, as revealed in Ephesians 2:6.

You and I are now channels through which (high elevations) the Spirit flows from to lift others up. According to the Scripture, "each of us in Christ are seated together with Him in heavenly places. That doesn't make us more valuable or better than others we are ministering to. It just gives us the privilege and responsibility to be channels He flows through – to lift up others from their low spiritual condition to their full *"new creation"* potential in Christ (2 Corinthians 5:17 ESV). Please notice, the distinction between Peter's message to the multitude on the Day of Pentecost:

> In Acts 2:17 KJV, *"And it shall come to pass in the last days, saith God, I will pour out of my Spirit upon all flesh …"* as he quotes a passage from (see Joel 2:28 KJV).

Peter was the first disciple to recognize the truth about Jesus (see Matthew 16:113-19). He was also the first to bear witness of Him. Peter began his sermon to men of Judea who had judged the whole occasion as being the results of too much wine (vv. 13, 15). In the OT passage (Joel 2:28-32), that Peter was quoting God had promised that a time was coming when all those who followed Him would receive His Spirit – not just the prophets, priests, kings, and judges. Peter pointed out that the time Joel prophesied about had come to pass. God would speak to and through all those who would come to Him, whether in visions, dreams or by prophecy. This was the beginning of the last days!

STUDY GUIDE: CHAPTER 3: UNDERSTANDING THE NEW COVENANT

1. From the start, no one in his or her own strength is able to live an _____ _____, free from sin's power and dominion.

2. Though the Spirit had not been poured out yet; God in His mercy gave His Spirit to those who have been called to do some _____ _____.

3. The children of Israel had no power to turn themselves around. This was the main concern with the Old Covenant, it demanded perfect obedience and complete turning around – but the _____ was not accompanied by the _____ _____ to obey.

4. Under the New Covenant God demands _____ _____ of His people.

5. Jesus taught His disciples that the _____ _____ would flow out of their innermost being (John 7:37-39).

6. The Holy Spirit was sent from heaven flowing into the earth – seeking out the _____ _____ of human suffering, weakness, and bondage.

7. Peter quoting God promised that a time was coming when all those who followed Him would have His Spirit in them – not just the _____, _____, _____, and judges.

CHAPTER FOUR

THE SEED PRINCIPLE

"The Sower sows the word, and these are those along the path, where the word is sown: when they hear, Satan immediately comes and takes away the word that is sown in them. And these are the ones sown on rocky ground: the ones who when they hear the word, immediately receive it with joy. And they have no root in themselves, but endure for a while; then, when tribulation or persecution arises on account of the word, immediately they fall away. And others are the ones sown among thorns. They are those who hear the word, but the cares of the world and the deceitfulness of riches and the desires for other things enter in and choke the word, and it proves unfruitful. But those that were sown on the good soil are the ones who hear the word and accept it and bear fruit, thirtyfold and sixtyfold, and a hundredfold" (Mark 4:14-20 ESV).

The parable of the Sower is a foundational kingdom teaching of Jesus. It is something that every Christian who desires to prosper in the kingdom of God *must learn*. These are foundational truths that we *must operate in* our daily life. The scriptures, Matthew 13, Mark 4, and Luke 8, all recorded the parable of the Sower. It must be understood in order to gain a clear understanding of the Bible. That is the reason so many Christians do not know how the kingdom of God works, therefore, they are dependent upon others to help them. Embracing these Scriptures will change your life. Here Jesus was talking about a man who took seed and just scattered them over the whole field. As he sowed, the seed landed on *four different types of ground.* Jesus continued to speak about how these four different types of ground responded so the seed (word) could germinate or not.

The purpose of the parable is not to make Agri-farmers. Jesus used this simple natural item (seed) to illustrate a spiritual truth. Mark 4:14 is the key to this entire parable: the Sower sows the word of God. This parable explains how the kingdom works – it works off the Word of God. Many people think there should be something deeper and more complex. The whole kingdom of God: The Christian life, your victories and successes as a gospel believer is as simple as taking the Word of God and sowing it in your heart. If you simply cooperate and let the Word of God germinate, change will happen. So, the way a physical seed in the natural realm reproduces itself can easily be compared to the way God's Word works in our lives.

Why a Seed?

There are extremely specific reasons why Jesus chose a seed to illustrate the way the Word of God works. In the natural realm, you would never expect a crop without preparing the ground, planting the seeds, watering, and caring for them. If you did not do these necessary things to grow a crop, surely you would not be surprised when the crop does not grow up. As this process is repeated year after year, we can expect a *natural* harvest. It is the same way in your *spiritual* life if these same steps are taken with the Word of God planted in your heart. Yet, Many Christians who have *never* planted the Word of God in their own heart are disappointed and surprised that they do not reap a *spiritual* harvest. They wonder,

- Why am I not healed?
- Why am I not financially prospering?
- Why hasn't God answered my prayer?
- Why are my relationships falling apart?
- Why can't I hold down a job?
- Why is it that nothing in my life seems to work?

They have been praying and asking God for these things, but they *have not taken His Word and promises and sown them in their heart* and *life* **by faith!** I have had people come to me over the years with these or similar questions. I ask them, what *Scriptures* are you standing on for being healed? That goes for all the above requests. What *promises* (seeds) of God's Word have you sown into your spirit and life to produce that healing, financial blessing, job, or relationship? Many respond with, "I don't know what the Word says, but I just know it's God's will. I believe God wants to heal me." They do not have a Scripture or promise to stand on. They did not sow His Word in their hearts.

The devil doesn't know what to do with a Christian who believes the Word of God! – Jay Leach

---

The number one reason people are not receiving from God is because they have not literally taken the truths of His Word and planted them in their hearts. This is why Jesus used this type of parable (the Sower and the seed). He wants us to understand how His kingdom works.

The Sower sows the Word of God. The seed He is talking about is not a physical seed. Rather, the Word of God is like a seed. Look up every passage of Scripture in the Bible pertaining to your need. Study the recorded scriptural examples where people were healed, or other needs were met.

Humble *yourself*

If you humble yourself and receive the truth, it will provide the answers to why you are not seeing more victory in your life than you are. It will also explain why you are not seeing more of the power of God at work. The average person is not meditating in the Word of God. They are not spending quality time in studying God's Word (be saturated with the Word like a sponge submerged in water).

The average Christian does not have an adequate understanding of the Word of God, especially a correct understanding of how the kingdom of God works. I know this is true because I deal with many people on a regular basis. They say, "My pastor said ..." or I believe the Bible says ..." That is not going to get you healed. So, you see, He has given you these seeds, but we have not planted them!

God has established natural laws, and He will not break them. You must plant seeds to produce a crop in the natural realm. Likewise, He has established spiritual laws, and He will not break those either. You cannot have victory in your life without the Word of God being planted in your heart! God's Word tell us that the Lord *"sent His word, and healed them, and delivered them from their destruction"* (Psalm107:20 ESV).

All through the Bible are promises revealing God as our Healer and Provider and attesting to how He wants to prosper us, but to see His healing and provision *you* must take God's Word and start planting it in your heart and life.

Your corporation

Notice in the parable of the Sower if you want certain kingdom results in your marriage, finances, relationships, health or whatever, the seeds (promises in God's Word) that speaks to your situation and plant them in your heart and life by faith. If you obediently nurture and take care of it, you will reap the fruit you are after. Sadly, most people will not follow this pattern. They wait until the bottom falls out, then they pray wanting God to give them a miracle to clean up the crisis. Have mercy Father!

People get offended and fall into unbelief if things do not turn out the way they thought they should. There is nothing wrong with the spiritual laws, but undoubtedly there was something wrong with me. I must go to the Word of God; I must take the seeds (promises) that speaks about the fruit I want to produce and begin to meditate on them. Over time, what I have desired comes to pass. Time is in God's hands!

Remember, it's the seed that produces the fruit – not the ground. It is the Word (seed) that brings the desired results. The ground does have a very important role to play. It can either allow the seed to produce to its fullest potential or it can hinder, choke, and stop the Word from working. It bears repeating, it is not the ground itself that produces the fruit – it is the seed! The four types of ground the seed was sown in earlier correspond with the four different types of hearts (of spiritual understanding) people have. The Word of God must be sown in your heart. I have noticed that in most churches, only about 25% of the people do all of the giving and serving that keeps the church going. That corresponds to the teaching of the parable. Only one in four types of people who had sown in their hearts actually begin to produce fruit.

I have observed the same thing in the Bread of Life Bible College which my wife and I founded 23 Years ago. About 25% of the students really take the Word of God to heart and then go out to change the world in their area of influence. Certainly, many more students graduate and make a mark, but it is about one in four who have the experience and teaching received at the Bread of Life: that are discipled, (matured), and then they go out and change (disciple) other people through the Word of God as well (see 2 Timothy 2:2).

Keep in mind, though only 25% of the seed sown brought forth much fruit – it was not the seed that was the problem. God's Word is an incorruptible seed. A seed has the power within to reproduce itself. Notice in the parable the good ground (heart) yielded to the seed, it is the one with a teachable hearing heart that receives the seed of the kingdom truth receives it and becomes fruitful.

What hindered three out of four from producing one-hundred-fold with their incorruptible seed (truth of the kingdom to be received and become fruitful)? The condition of the ground (heart) into which the seed is sown makes the difference. In the case of understanding in the hearts. Notice the parable of the Sower in Matthew 13:18-23,

- Hard ground (the word is received by the wayside (the ground is packed foot traffic doesn't penetrate the soil) (see v.19).
- Stony ground (receives the seed but has no roots in himself) (see vv. 20-21).
- Thorny ground (receives the word but the cares of the world choke it out and it becomes unfruitful) (see v.22).

- Good ground is he who hears the word, receives it, and understands it, and applies – it is this person (heart) who indeed bears fruit and produces: some a hundredfold, some sixty, some thirty (see v. 23).

Where is the local Church in all of this?

Our website describes the Bread of Life as a Christian ministry that helps people grow in Jesus Christ as they move through life. Additionally, it says that "We spread the Good News of Jesus Christ by establishing life-on-life mentoring or discipling – relationships with people, equipping them to make an impact on those who around them for God's glory." Having said that, it is interesting that this statement describes what churches should be doing!

Some people are concerned about parachurch ministries like the Bread of Life replacing the church. *Para* means *beside,* and it's reasonable to ask whether these parachurch ministries really work beside churches or *apart* from them.

If it is not wise to do disciple-making without a church – but it's worse to do church without disciple-making! Jay Leach

---

Yet isn't that the case with many local churches today? Christians join churches, and no one comes alongside them. The church has no culture of singles living with families to learn how to serve the Lord. Little hospitality. Only an occasional invite to Sunday dinner. Few men shepherding their wives and children, and no wives or older women generally discipling the younger women. No biblical counseling among the members themselves. In fact, counseling occurs only in offices. No one would think of going to a church where the style of music may not suit their taste, even though it serves and blesses others. No thought of helping a family who is homeless due to some natural disaster, to COVID-19, unemployed, hungry or some other life shattering crisis.

With churches like this, it's no wonder that so many people are now turning to parachurch ministries. Their experience has taught them that the local church is the last place to look for discipling opportunities.

The church as the disciple – maker

The Bible *teaches* that the local church is the *natural* environment for disciple-making (discipling). As a matter of fact, it teaches that the local church *is itself* the basic discipler of Christians. The church does this through *its weekly gatherings* and its *accountability structures* as well as its ministers and its members. These in turn provide the context for the consideration of one-on-one discipling:

- The gathered church is responsible to preach the whole counsel of God through those called, anointed, and gifted for this purpose.
- Through baptism the church affirms credible professions of faith.
- Through the Lord's Supper the church declares the Lord's death and resurrection – making the many into one.
- Through excommunication the church removes anyone whose life unrepentantly contradicts his or her profession

---

Genuine love transforms what we believe – into how we live!

Here then is the church's skeletal structure. Next we reach the relationships, which are the flesh and muscles. Living together now as one, the members of the church practice loving one another as Jesus has loved them:

> *"A new commandment I give to you, that you love one another: just as I have loved you, you also are to love one another: just as I have loved you, you also are to love one another. By this all people will know that you are my disciples, if you have love for one another"* (John 13:34-35 ESV).

Jesus' command to love was new because He gave it a new standard. Moses said, "Love your neighbor as yourself" (see Lev. 19:18). Jesus said the new standard was "as I have loved you." Jesus gave His disciples the example of love that they were to follow (see John 13:1-17). Jesus loved His disciples with a love that continually pointed to the words of His Father. That assured them of place being prepared for them. The local church is the primary disciple-maker of all Christians. The churches work begins by gathering together. The author of Hebrews writes, "And let us consider how to stir up one another to love and good works, not neglecting to meet together, as is the habit of some, but encouraging one another, and all the more as you see the Day drawing near"(10:24-25 ESV).

A Church that ministers out of the love of Christ first
and love its community second!

It is important to note here, the goal is to help "one another" follow Jesus. By not neglecting meeting together. By gathering! This was by Jesus' design! This month marks two years since the coronavirus closed the doors of the church. How long will the church stand by waiting to see? See what? Why we cannot wait! "We must get back to assembling ourselves together." Everyday some new evil *advances* in our cities and communities across America.

Fasting still brings deliverance and victory

Today our national and international leaders are making rash decisions many times without consulting with colleagues and when considering consultation their mind is already made up – for their own good. Diplomacy is out. Innocent people are being killed by selfish villains, who could care less what the age of the victim is. Then there are national emergencies, namely our current conflicts with Russia and China in both cases the lines are being drawn and armed forces are massing. At the same time depending on whose report you read, after two years with COVID-19, we still could possibly be facing something far worse by the variants which are crisscrossing the globe presently many claiming them to be far worse.

If we turn to the historical records of the Old Testament, we find a number of occasions where **collective fasting** and **prayer** brought forth dramatic and powerful intervention by God. One occasion that comes to my mind found in 2 Chronicles 20:1-30. Jehoshaphat, the king of Judah received word that a very large army comprised of forces from Moab, Ammon, and Mount Seir combined was invading his kingdom from the east. Realizing that he had no military resources with which to meet the challenge, Jehoshaphat turned to God for help!

His first decisive act is described in verse 3: *"Jehoshaphat ... proclaimed a fast throughout all Judah" (KJV).* In this way, God's people were called to unite in public, collective fasting, and prayer for divine intervention. We see in verse 13 that men, women, and children were included. From this initial fasting, events followed in swift succession, leading up to a dramatic climax. The first result is recorded in verse

4: *"And Judah gathered themselves together, to ask help of the LORD; even out of all the cities of Judah they came to seek the LORD" (KJV).* **Common danger** had the effect of bringing all of God's people together. The same emergency threatened each community or city all alike. No doubt there were jealousies or rivalries between some of the represented cities. But in the face of the enemy invasion, those differences were set aside: **God's people were called upon to protect their common inheritance rather than to promote their individual differences.**

With the people of Judah in one accord, Jehoshaphat led them in a prayer, reminding God of His covenant with Abraham and His promises of mercy based on that covenant. **Jehoshaphat's prayer received an immediate, supernatural response from God,** which is described in verses 14 through 17. Through one of the Levites presents named Jahaziel, the Holy Spirit gave forth a powerful prophetic utterance, combining encouragement, assurance, and direction.

Jahaziel's prophetic utterance was received in turn with spontaneous worship and praise by Jehoshaphat and all the people. Thereafter, Jehoshaphat organized praise as he led his people forth to battle:

> *And Jehoshaphat bowed his head with his face to the ground: and all Judah and the inhabitants of Jerusalem fell before the LORD, worshipping the LORD. And the Levites stood up to praise the LORD God of Israel with a loud voice on high…. And when he [Jehoshaphat] had consulted with the people, he appointed singers unto the LORD, and that should praise the beauty of holiness, as they went out before the army, and to say, Praise the LORD for his mercy endureth forever* (2 Chron. 20:18-19, 21 KJV).

The outcome is described in verses 22 through 30. There was no need for God's people to use any kind of military weaponry. **The entire army of their enemies destroyed themselves leaving not one survivor.**

All that God's people needed to do was to spend three days gathering the spoils and then return in triumph to Jerusalem, with their voices raised in loud thanksgiving and praise to God. Furthermore, the impact of this tremendous, supernatural victory was felt by all the surrounding nations. From that time on, no other nation dared to even think about hostilities against Jehoshaphat and his people.

Three practical lessons can be learned from Jehoshaphat's victory. All three lessons apply equally to Christians in this day and age:

1. The anti-Christian forces that are at work in the world today are just as hostile and just as fierce as the army that threatened Jehoshaphat and Judah. This is not the time for Christians to emphasize issues that divide us. Rather, it is time for all God's people to follow Judah's example and unite in fasting and prayer.

2. The story of Jehoshaphat demonstrates the need for spiritual gifts. It was the gift of *prophecy* that gave both encouragement and direction to Judah in their hour of crisis. The gifts of the Spirit are needed just as much today as ever. In the book of Acts, Peter quoted the prophecy of Joel and applied it to our present age (see Acts 2:17-18).

3. The third lesson to be learned from this story of Jehoshaphat is the supremacy of spiritual power over carnal power. In 2 Corinthians 10:4, Paul said, *"For the weapons of our warfare are not carnal, but mighty through God"* (KJV).

There are two kinds of weapons: spiritual and carnal: Jehoshaphat's enemies relied on carnal weapons; Jehoshaphat and his people used spiritual weapons. The outcome of the conflict demonstrates the absolute supremacy of the spiritual over the carnal. What exactly were the spiritual weapons that Jehoshaphat used so effectively? They may be briefly summarized as follows:

1. Collective fasting
2. United prayer
3. The supernatural gifts of the Holy Spirit
4. Public worship and praise

These weapons, scripturally employed by Christians in the present day, will gain victories as powerful and dramatic as they gained for the people of Judah in the days of Jehoshaphat.

STUDY GUIDE: CHAPTER 4 THE SEED PRINCIPLE

1. The parable of the Sower is foundational to kingdom teaching of Jesus. These are foundational truths that we must operate our daily life. The Scriptures, Matthew 13, Mark 4, and Luke 8, all recorded the parable of the Sower. It *must* be understood in order to gain a clear understanding of the Bible.

2. Jesus used this simple natural item (seed) to illustrate a spiritual truth. Mark 4:14 is the key to this entire parable. The Sower sows the word of God. It works off the Word of God. You are to sow the word of God into your heart. If you corporate and let the Word germinate, change will happen.

3. So, the way a physical seed in the natural realm reproduces itself can easily be compared to the way God's Word works in our lives.

4. The number one reason people are not receiving from God is because they have not literally taken the truths of God's Word and planted them in their hearts.

5. Explain the four types of ground and seed (see Matthew 13:18-23)

6. Jesus' command to love was new because He gave it a new standard. He said the new standard was _____ __ _____ _____ _____.

7. There are two kinds of weapons spiritual and carnal. Jehoshaphat's spiritual weapons proved to be superior to the enemies carnal weapons.

CHAPTER FIVE

I appeal to you therefore, brothers, by the mercies of God, to present your bodies as a living sacrifice, holy and acceptable to God, which is your spiritual worship. Do not be conformed to this world, but be transformed by the renewal of your mind, that by testing you may discern what is the will of God, what is good and acceptable and perfect" (Romans 12:1-2 ESV).

Our obedience to God is more than merely the fulfillment of duty; it is the means of our experiencing personal happiness (see John 3:17), our pleasing God (see 1 John 3:22), and our expressing our love for Him (see John 14:15, 21, 23). Simply telling God that we love Him may just be sentimentalism – but God searches our hearts and lives as well as listen to our words for true expressions of our love for Him.

Despite Satan's lies, obedience to God is not grievous (see 1 John 5:3), but good for us, suitable to our **1)** renewed minds and bodies, **2)** new nature, and **3)** born again spirits (see Romans 12:2). Our obedience to God requires *that we learn His will for us in everything* *and — that we do it in His way and His time. God's will for His children is His Word.* Please grasp these truths!

1. God's commands are *directed to our will — not to our emotions!*
2. He never relieves us of our assigned calling — because we do not feel like doing it or do not want to do it.
3. God's will for His people today is found in the commands, appeals and principles in the Bible.

It is imperative that all true Christians living know that service begin with personal dedication and commitment to the Lord. It has been said, the Christian who fails in life is the one who first failed at the altar — refusing to completely surrender to Christ. King Saul failed at the altar, and it cost him his kingdom (see 1 Sam. 13:8 and 15:10). Love is the motive for dedication. Paul did not command you, but he said, "I beseech of what God has already done for you." We serve Christ out of love and appreciation. True dedication is the presenting of spirit, soul [mind, emotions, and will], and the body holistically to God:

1. yielding the body to Him, daily,
2. renewing the mind daily by the Word of God, and
3. daily surrendering the will through prayer and obedience.

Shaping our Will

When we give ourselves to the Lord, we express our willingness to comply with His will and commands (see Matthew 11:29). Our commitment to God requires us to stop following the world's evil lifestyles, godless way of thinking, and attitudes. Again, to conform to the world is to assume a lifestyle that is contrary to our agreement with what we are as the people of God (see Eph. 2:10) and is not in keeping with our commitment toward Christlikeness and eternal life (see Eph. 5:1-18; Col. 3:8-17; Gal. 6:7-8).

Therefore, we constantly transform[10] to God's will. Having Jesus in us, we must allow Him to manifest Himself in our attitudes, character, and actions (see Gal. 2:20; 4:19). We do this daily by giving ourselves to Him and by following the biblical moral lifestyle that portrays Him (study carefully Rom. 13:14; Eph. 5:1-18; Col.3:1-14; Matt. 5:48). Thus, we must learn God's will and willingly commit to doing it in the power of the Holy Spirit and the Word, for the glory of God.

Every Christian is either a *conformer,* living for the world, or a *transformer,* daily becoming more and more like Christ. The Gk. Word for "transform" is the same as the one for "transfigure" in (Matthew 17:2 ESV). Transform means outwardly expressing an inner reality. Paul tells us that we are transformed (transfigured) as we allow the Spirit to reveal Christ through the Word of God (see 2 Corinthians 3:18 ESV).

It is only when the Christian is thus personally transformed and dedicated to God that he or she can know God's will for their life! Romans12:2 says, "We are transformed by the renewing of our minds."[11] There was a time in America when the majority of people held a body of opinion to be true. For example, there existed a solid belief of right and wrong. Today, there are many different religions in this country brought on through import and multiculturalism. Each on their own journey to truth, but the desired destination has not changed.

---

[10] Transform means outwardly expressing an inner reality.

[11] The renewing of the mind [one of four components that make up the soul] is the total interchange of our ideas, perceptions, images, and feelings for those of Christ. Bill Hull *Choose the Life* (Baker Books, Grand Rapids, Mich. 2004) 102-103

> "For who has understood the mind of the Lord so as to instruct him?" But we have the mind of Christ" (1 Cor. 2:16 ESV).

Likewise, does God have three wills – of which we just choose one? No, no, as we grow in love and obedience to God, so our love of His will, grows. Some Christians obey because they fear His chastening. Others obey because they find God's will acceptable. However, we find the deepest disciples are those who love God's will and find it perfect.

Spiritual Sacrifices (Hebrews 13:11-16)

As New Testament priests, we are to present "spiritual sacrifices" to God (1 Peter 2:5 ESV).

A spiritual sacrifice is something done or given in the name of Christ and for His glory (see Hebrews 13:15).

A spiritual sacrifice is something done or given in the name of God and for His glory. In Hebrews 13:15, the writer states that "praise" is such a sacrifice. "Good works" and "sharing material blessings" are also spiritual sacrifices (v. 16). Other spiritual sacrifices include "the believer's body" (see Romans 12:1-2); "offerings" (see Phil. 4:18); "prayer" (see Ps. 141:2); "a broken heart" (see Ps. 51:17); and "discipleship" (2 Timothy 2:2):

We must choose the life – the life of discipleship as practiced and taught by Jesus and lived out by His first century followers. We must courageously cast off our "non-discipleship Christianity, and submit ourselves to a life of accountability, personal transformation, and making disciples, to do anything less is failure. The greatest omission is the Great Commission.[12]

Christ's plan of multiplication

If we are to restore Christ's plan of discipleship to our local churches, first, we must start with a fuller understanding of what the disciples heard from Jesus when He commanded them to "Go, make disciples." Undoubtedly, the disciples gathered that Jesus said they should go and find people *like themselves* and develop them to follow Jesus, who in turn would commit to do the same to others (only a disciple can make a disciple). Years later the Apostle Paul no doubt passed this commitment on to his spiritual son, Timothy, when he wrote, "And the things that you have heard from me among many witnesses, commit these to faithful men who will be able to teach others also" (2 Tim. 2:2 NKJV). This is the guiding Scripture of the Bread of Life Ministries Int'l. Disciple-making has been our task for 23 years.

Jesus says, "Follow Me." Let us explore the magnitude of who it is we are called to follow. As we discover how God transforms disciples of Jesus from the inside out, we will see the Christian life as an overwhelming delight. To say that you believe in Jesus *apart* from conversion in your life completely *misses* the essence of what it means to follow Jesus. Let no one fool you, your relationship with Jesus and your position before God are not based on a decision you made, a prayer you prayed, or a card you signed. When it is all over, we will find ourselves joined with brothers and sisters the world over

---

[12] Bill Hull, *"Choose the Life"* (Baker Books, Grand Rapids, MI 2004) 42

accomplishing a grand purpose that God set in motion before the foundation of the world was set.

The Word of God faces violent opposition today. As ministers of the Most High God, we are to minister the Word boldly and courageously. We are to treasure it and defend it tirelessly – always being careful to communicate its truth with accuracy and purity (these also are spiritual sacrifices). It is imperative that you train others to do the same. Be strong in grace, drawing deeply on God's enabling power and anointing to accomplish His purpose in and through you.

Reproduction

You don't have to understand everything to get God's Word working in your life. Just start sowing the Word into your heart (not your head). God put life in those seeds with the power to reproduce themselves. Begin meditating on the Word of God, day, and night. The Word will germinate, take root, spring forth, and grow up of itself.

How did God put life into those seeds? Man cannot figure out, but the Word of God tells us that God spoke life into physical seeds. Likewise, He spoke life into the spiritual seed of His Word. Even though I cannot explain it all that does not keep me from cooperating and reaping the benefits of it. Proverbs 4:20-22 says:

> *"My son, attend to my words; incline thine ear unto my sayings.*
> *Let them not depart from thine eyes; keep them*
> *in the midst of thine heart.*
> *For they are life unto those that find,*
> *and health to all their flesh.*

God's Word contains His life in it. If you would take His words, His sayings, and put them on the inside of you, then God's kind of life would start flowing through you. You will find that healing, prosperity, joy, peace – everything Jesus provided are in God's Word. The Bible is not like any other book even books about the Bible. The difference is – it is alive!

> *"For the word of God is quick, and powerful,*
> *and sharper than any two-edged sword."*
> Hebrews 4:12

By Faith

When I was a little boy, one day I dug up a little area of the backyard, perhaps 6" x 6" and planted some radish seeds I found in daddy's toolshed. I could hardly wait to get home from school the next day to check and see if the radishes were ready for harvest. Low and behold they had not even burst through the ground yet. So, after 4 days I gave up, thinking the seeds must have been too old and abandoned my 1st agricultural project.

Sometime later after forgetting my project, I happened to be passing that little patch in the yard and to my surprise there was a clump of radishes ready for harvest. I proudly pulled them up and went and presented them to my mom! I often think of the life lessons my mother taught me on that occasion about seeds, seasons, patience, and faith.

It is the same with the Word of God. You cannot just select a promise, plant it, and expect to reap a harvest instantly. A couple of days later you bring it up and nothing has happened – you repeat the process each day for the next week. Well, nothing is happening. And then you decide to go back one more time, you go, and nothing has happened. That certainly is not abiding in the Word, nor letting the Word abide in you (see John 15:5). Because you keep digging it up you will not see it produce. You take the Word of God, put it in your heart, leave it there, meditate on it, and it produces. You must realize that seed, time, and harvest are all parts of the process. Reaching the harvest takes time.

STUDY GUIDE: CHAPTER 5 LEARNNG AND DOING GOD'S WILL

1. Our _____ to God is more than merely the fulfillment of duty; it is the means of our experiencing _____ _____ (see John 3:17).

2. God's commands are directed to our will, not to our _____.

3. God's will for His people today is found in the commands, appeal, and principles in the Bible.

4. Love is the motive for _____.

5. When we give ourselves to the Lord, we express our _____ to comply with His _____ and commands (see Matthew 11:29).

6. Only when the Christian is personally transformed and dedicated to God can he or she knows _____ _____ for their life (see Romans 12:2).

7. As New Testament priests, we are to present _____ _____ to God (see 1 Peter 2:5).

CHAPTER SIX
HOLISTIC MINISTRY (A STRATEGY)

"And we all, with unveiled face beholding the glory of the Lord, are being transformed into the same image from one degree of glory to another. For this comes from the Lord who is the Spirit" (2 Corinthians 3:18 ESV).

Ministry does not mean perfect people, rather, we recognize we are all on a journey of transformation together, from one degree of glory to another. The future of the church is in trouble, and those of us who teach need to step up and accept our share of blame. God has entrusted us with a high and holy calling, but we have treated it like it is just another mundane task.

Our carelessness in teaching God's Word should haunt us daily, as we witness the incredibly high number of youth and young adults of this generation who call themselves Christians but use the term differently than most of us do.

And the survey says

Survey after survey have shown that many young people raised in church going Christian families have abandoned their faith by the time they are senior high schoolers and/or early college. We have witnessed educational, governmental, recreational, and familial masses walk away from the faith. For decades subtle changes to many distinctive norms differentiated the average churchgoing family from those families outside the church, however, the unconventional has become the normal as the conventional family is decreasing across both segments of American family life today by:

- More blended families
- More single parents sharing the children on alternate weekends
- More gay and lesbian couples raising children
- More twenty and thirtysomething singles cohabitation
- More diverse ideas about what family means

The orientation of church programming toward a shrinking family demographic will prove to be a challenge for many local Christian churches because they do not know how *to disciple* the rapidly growing number of unconventional, unmarried, overcommitted, nontraditional families. Though the coronavirus rages all churches should realize our lack of preparation in this matter and the profound implications for the choices we make about ministry. We will further discuss this topic in a later chapter. But keep heart, God has revealed, just as He did to Elijah, "seven thousand in Israel, "all the knees that have not bowed to Baal" (1 Kings 19:18 ESV).

A company called Highway Video in Mountain View, California provides more evidence that has produced a series of film shorts, some "person to person on the street" interviews asking basic questions about Christianity. These anonymous interviewees reflect an alarming lack of understanding about the God of the Bible, even among those who grew up in church. All leading to the conclusion that the church has done a poor job making disciples of most of the teenagers God has directed to them.

We must do a better job of passing on the faith (see Jude 3). We cannot just tell young people today what they are to believe. Additionally, we have to do more than just make sure that they feel close to God. These strategies have played out.

What is Holistic Ministry?

The best strategy for raising the next generation of Christian disciples is to teach them holistically to:

- Feed their souls
- Challenge their minds
- Strengthen their emotions
- Guide their actions and behavior

All through the [Inward] power of the Holy Spirit and the Word of God working in tandem. We see this type of holistic ministry teaching in the Scriptures. *The whole gospel for the whole person [holistically].*

The root meaning of the word "holistic" is whole, from the Greek "hollos." Realizing that the world is broken and far short of the glory God intended in the very beginning. Through holistic ministry the church responds to the world's brokenness by proclaiming and modeling a right relationship with God in Christ and participating in the ongoing Kingdom work of personal and social restoration. As Christ is making us whole individually and corporately, God's Spirit works through us [the Church of Jesus Christ] to bring wholeness to others. The whole gospel brings salvation in its entirety:

- Repentance
- forgiveness of sins
- regeneration
- transformation
- physical and emotional healing
- social and economic (recovery and restoration)
- reconciliation and peace

Holistic ministry can be summarized as: Reaching your community with the whole gospel for the whole person through whole churches.[13]

Holistic ministry takes place in holistic congregations, where disciples of Christ are made and live out their salvation in loving fellowship. Ministry does not perfect people who have it all together, but recognize we are all on a journey of transformation (Christlikeness) together "from one degree of glory to another" (see 2 Cor. 3:18). Realizing that each of us have made a contribution to the pain, suffering and decay in the world.

Thus, I serve admitting my own brokenness before a holy God, acknowledging the fact that the benefit my ministering Christ's wholeness to others helps to make me whole. Praise God! Jay Leach

---

A holistic approach also mean that the whole church works together toward a unifying ministry that utilizes the spiritual gifts of each disciple. All Christians are to bear fruit as branches of the larger

---

[13] Accessed 4/26/21 (https//christiansforsocialaction.org)

vine (see 1 Cor. 12:20). Conversely, each individual congregation needs the ministry of the whole Christian Community. We are called to reach our whole communities with the *whole gospel for the whole person* through whole churches. Walking in the Spirit daily as they live out the whole gospel with much emphasis on disciple-making and a passion for outreach.

Holistic ministry entails more than sponsoring a program now and then. It goes beyond short-term aid relief. It means modeling God's concern for the total well-being of individuals and communities. It means walking in newness of life, an incarnational transformed lifestyle of integrity, compassion, and incitement. It means sharing the good news of both justification and going on in sanctification in transformation (full mature discipleship).

Again, the church is God's chosen vessel for modeling Christ and the Good News of Christ in our world. Yes, this is how Christ meant His followers to live, love and serve together. Holistic ministry means loving neighbors both far and near with the same joy that Jesus displayed, especially to those who are most needy and least lovable. The source of holistic ministry remains, God's redeeming and transformational power!

Morals and Values

When we study morals and values, ideologically, the people outside of the church are different from many who regularly attend. However, this distinctiveness emerges during any discussion of moral values, which must be touched on due to the basis of those moral choices. For a disciple of Jesus, the Bible without a doubt is the standard on which morals are based. But what about those do not have a *biblical foundation* upholding their morality? Statistics reflect that half of the nation's people outside of the church make their moral decisions based on *their feelings about right and wrong*. Then there are those who say they do not know what it means for anything to be "morally right, so they just do the best they can in whatever situation. We can see that in this situation things can go either way; the church has no choice in the matter accept the Bible standard. Many churches are in trouble today because they decided to make exceptions.

Launching Your Holistic ministry

Launching a new ministry can be a personally rewarding experience. *Intentional preparation* to enter the ministry will pay off not only by increasing the ways that God can use you to be a blessing to others, but also by cultivating the soil of your own walk in the Spirit for God's ongoing work in you. Some of the ways are these:

- Stand on the truth of God's Word.
- Expressing Christian love (1 John 3:16-18; 1 Cor. 13:4-7).
- Being an example (1 Tim. 4:12; 1 Cor. 11:1; Phil. 3:17; 3-9).
- Praying (2 Cor. 1:11; Eph. 6:18-19).
- Encouraging others and reproof (1 Thess. 5:1 Heb. 10:24; Gal. 6:1).
- Exercising your spiritual gifts such as pastoral care; teaching and showing mercy (1 Cor. 14:26; Eph. 4:12-16).
- Giving bodily or material assistance (1 Cor. 16:1; Gal. 6:10; Phil. 4:15-16).

Are you allowing others to minister to you? One of the hindrances to effective ministry in our churches is the prevalence of arrogance over godly humility. If this fits you, ask the Lord to help you to get it right. Are you willing to learn from others who, may not be as for along in their spiritual growth as you are? Do not neglect giving them the opportunity (see Heb. 10:14-15). Thank God for the people in your church's holistic ministries to your life.

STUDY GUIDE: CHAPTER 6 HOLISTIC MINISTRY (A STRATEGY)

1. Holistic ministry can be summarized as: reaching your community with the whole gospel for the whole person through whole churches.

2. Thus, we serve admitting our own brokenness before a Holy God, acknowledging the fact that the benefit of our ministering Christ's wholeness to others helps to make us whole.

3. The church is God's chosen _____ for modeling Christ and the _____ _____ of Christ in our world.

4. In the matter of determining what is right or wrong morally, the church has no choice in the matter accept the _____ _____.

5. Stand in the truth of God's Word!

6. One of the major hinderances to _____ _____ in our churches is the prevalence of arrogance over godly humility.

7. Are you allowing others to minister to you?

CHAPTER SEVEN
THE MINISTER AS SHEPHERD

"My anger is hot against the shepherds, and I will punish the leaders; for the LORD of hosts cares for his flock, the house of Judah, and will make them like his majestic steed in battle" (Zechariah 10:3 ESV).

For too long, we have neglected the biblical leadership model that God has both authorized and demonstrated. Repeatedly God referred to the leaders of Israel as shepherds. It has been said that we can glean leadership principles by studying the errors of Israel's shepherds. However, when you examine the text carefully, you see that God did not rebuke these men for leading the flock astray – but for not caring! Their sin was not poor leadership but poor shepherdship. Because these shepherds did not care, their sheep wandered off [STRAYED AWAY]. It was **not** that these leaders:

- lacked a vision for the future.
- failed to inspire confidence in the people.

- abandoned good management principles.
- disregarded sound leadership principles.
- neglected to hear what the people were telling them.
- They **didn't care** for the sheep.

The fuel that kindled this fire was that they didn't care for the sheep. That is what God says burned ancient Israel to the ground. Today some pastors describe themselves as CEO's, managers, and even the boss, but just in case we forgot the critical importance God attaches to this *shepherd's role,* let me end this section with a repeat reference to the prophet Zechariah (see Zech. 10:1-3), a priest born in the Babylonian exile returned to Judah in 538 B.C. with Zerubbabel, a descendant of David, and others to rebuild the Jerusalem temple.

The problem of these ancient shepherds was not so much their serving, as that they **failed to care**. Since it is possible to serve without caring, the apostle Paul gave a very fitting warning for not only his day, but for us today: "If I give away all I have, and if I deliver up my body to be burned, but **have not love**, I gain nothing" (1 Cor. 13:1 ESV). Emphasis added. You might ask, "How is this possible?" Because one can do all that and still "have not love." All of us called into the pastorate must ask ourselves: *Do we care for the sheep?* Certainly, we all get frustrated or irritated with the sheep at times – but even that comes because we care for them. Jesus gave us the proper pattern to follow. God's heart is grieved at what His sheep sometimes do and don't do.

From the Scriptures we see that Jesus Christ, the Great Shepherd grieves over His sheep. Likewise, our hearts will be grieved as well. Paul wrote to the Corinthian Church, which was particularly difficult to deal with:

> "*I fear that perhaps when I come, I may find you not as*
> *I wish, and that you may find me not as you wish – that*

perhaps there may be quarreling, jealousy, anger, hostility, slander, gossip, conceit, and disorder. I fear that when I come again my God may humble me before you, and I may have to mourn over many of those who sinned earlier and have not repented of the impurity, sexual immorality, and sensuality that have been practiced" (2 Corinthians 12:20,21 ESV).

Counterculture

There are many things that require change, if the church is going to remain relevant, that is, to be a counterculture in a world that is in league with the antichrist spirit. Ministers at all levels especially pastors must step up to the plate and realize that without Christ we can do nothing. Those who specialize in sin-management as is the case in many local churches today should follow Paul's lead in countering false apostles and false ministers whose intent is to lead the church astray from the pure truth, the pure Gospel (see 2 Cor. 12:13-15). He fears that he may find eight (continued) sins among the Corinthians when he arrive for a visit. It is certainly his desire that they be cleaned up before he arrives. Being a realist, Paul called these wrong things by their right names (see vv. 20-21):

1. Quarreling
2. Jealousy
3. Anger
4. Tumults
5. Slander
6. Selfishness
7. Pride
8. Licentiousness

The second *time around*

Across the spectrum of the American church today, the unashamed immorality and temptation that was present in the Corinthian Church, when Paul made his second visit is presently here today. The church must come out of hiding behind the four walls and become the offensive countercultural that God intended! Let him who boasts, boast of the Lord, so says Paul. No Christian should dare boast of his own efforts of success. All that we have been able to do in God's *service he* has done it in us and through us. *Both the call and the power are His!* This is a fundamental humility which alone can exalt us (see Luke 18:14).

Today the craving for prestige, money, the love of power and the conceit in people that makes them feel that they alone are responsible for the body and souls of people create jealousies that cause friction, much unhappiness and turn the ministry into a competitive struggle. Paul's fear for the Corinthian Church was that wholehearted devotion to Christ might be altered and a false Christianity might supplant the true faith. This is truly the challenge for our churches today across America and the West.

A sincere and pure devotion to the person of Jesus Christ is the secret of true Christianity.

Another Jesus

Seduction was already at work. False ministers had come into the church to plant their destructive ideas. They preached a different Jesus than the Jesus Paul preached. This was crucial then and even more so today as false ministers continue to preach another gospel. The Christian faith (see Jude 3) is based on devotion to Jesus, the Son of God, who *"became flesh and dwelt among is,"* who was crucified, who rose from the dead, and now reigns as Lord at God's right hand. A show of His validity came when He asked His disciples who accompanied Him daily, *"Who do you say that I am?"* (see Matthew 16:15). They had seen His glory and had only one explanation. Peter spoke up, *"You are the Christ, the Son of the living God."* Upon this faith and devotion His church would be built.

A different Jesus, one who was merely the head of the Jewish people, or as some religions claim today, merely a teacher, or a social reformer, or just a good man, but is not the Jesus of the Christian faith. This falsity shows up in the many religions so prevalent in America today. Sadly, any such picture of Jesus then and now robs the true gospel of its meaning and its power. Compromising for a different Jesus today has created a different spirit in the church, such as was seen in the Judaizers in Corinth, who rejected Christian freedom and sought to restore the chains of Jewish legalism. To summarize, a different Jesus produces:

- A different spirit in the church
- A different gospel
- Good advice instead good news
- Presents an ideal instead of power
- Substitutes legalism for grace
- Substitutes works and legal observances
- Rejects salvation by faith in Jesus Christ

Human leadership

Many false leaders are offering *another* Christ today, stripped of His glory as the incarnate Son of God has no earthly significance. He cannot answer our most perplexing questions, such as the meaning of life:

- The nature of God
- Man's final destiny

Paul is both sad and upset that the Corinthian Church or any part of it, should have been so easily persuaded by these false leaders. That such immoralities should find their way into the church is a possibility hard to accept. However, the Christian faith does not rest on a sentimental belief in human goodness. It rest on the knowledge of the inherent sinfulness of human nature apart from redeeming grace. This fact makes the gospel both credible and necessary.

New Testament power [body] ministers

Looking at Paul and the Corinthian Church above, we see many similarities in the 21st Century church in America today. In I Corinthians 12, 13, 14 we are introduced to what I call, New Testament power [body] ministers. For centuries many ministers and churches have operated on the belief that the body of Christ no longer need apostles, prophets, and teachers once the whole Bible was completed (New Testament). Paul describes the dilemma of *(bondage of the flesh)* humanity in Romans 7, even though we now have the New Testament. He or she is unable to move into the *(spiritual freedom)* of Romans 8, where power over the dominion of sin is revealed. The Word of God working in tandem with the Holy Spirit promises hope, and empowerment to win over temptations, sin, and lusts.[14] Once a person receives salvation, the Holy Spirit enters and encourages the new Christian to *go deeper in the faith* (Jude 3) and urges him or her to reproduce themselves in others.

The idea that *there is a deeper and better spiritual life* than most Christians know or are aware of on this resurrection side of the cross.

---

[14] For a deep study and explanation of this transformation see my book *The Apostolic Rising* (Trafford Publishing 2021) xiv, 83.

This is a **crucial message** during this COVID-19 hour in time. The unsaved are crying and hurting over circumstances they have no way of controlling. While many of us who are saved may be going through the same circumstances, we *have Jesus!* If there was ever a time that we need to stand strong and share Him with others – this is the day! Like the Corinthian Church, over time the American Christian church has moved from the center of God's will to the outer extremes [externalism].

Over the years many "experts" have suggested a variety of cures for the church's ailments. They spoke and we hit the bookstores to buy their books and attend their seminars and conferences that promised to lead us into great success and growth. Strangely, with all of this help the American church continues to *decline,* at the same time we invest in more resources designed to make us more effective as pastors and to help our churches *impact* the world for Christ. Another group would show up and conclude that, you don't know how to manage the ministry or the budget. We can show you how. Promises, promises, and more promises – of course these church experts failed to tell us that the people in the business world from whom they took their theories already knew that didn't work. These "experts" never repent and return to say, "I'm sorry." But many will return and claim the church was lacking in faith, so, I brought along with me today, another strategy.

Today many have moved both pastors and churches from a community model to a corporation model. In some churches the pastors preach good and leave the business side of things to someone else. In other churches the pastor is the CEO, the boss, the chairperson of the board. The pastor then is a corporate officer instead of a shepherd.

First of all, in such churches the Holy Spirit with His power, gifts, and ministries have been replaced with traditions of men, programs, external forms and ceremonies. These changes were affected over several generations. Rather than seeking the Spirit's guidance day by day, many pastors and churches became content with what they did yesterday and last year. Such churches still exist today – looking backward and repeating *is* a learned behavior. Much of this behavior is placed above the Word of God in importance. These churches become weak and ineffective for kingdom work.

Today is the day for (?) in the church

Sadly, we are experiencing a phenomenon in the churches during the coronavirus with many churches are still closed while sports events and beaches are welcoming thousands of people daily. We are seeing the governments at state and national level at odds over mask mandates. Also we are saddled with the utter confusion of conspiracy theories gone wild.

It seems that a spirit of fear and numbness has overshadowed the Christian community in this country. With the absence of Dr. Billy Graham or one like him to speak into the hearts of the people – media and politics seem to have a free hand with the people. The church finds herself pursuing many noteworthy and necessary pursuits while laying aside the one that *only the church can do – proclaim the gospel of our salvation to a dying world.* Many of our pastors and other church leaders have succumbed to partisan politics; which further separate the people. Other agencies will assist the poor or stand against injustice – but no other agency will preach the gospel. Certainly the church must do her part to counter poverty and oppression – but these should never become the main function of the church. We must protect and proclaim the gospel of Jesus Christ.

Partisan politics has large parts of the church in America favoring individualism and separation producing a divided church culture that is being walloped from all sides by traditionalism, progressivism, liberalism, conservatism, multiculturism, secularism, atheism, and even politicians are striving to put their individual views and priorities above biblical principles, standards, and practices.

Whose vision should we follow?

Many Christians in the past thirty or forty years have said, "Pastor I want to believe what you are telling us. I want to follow you in the direction we need to go. But understand this: I've been at this church thirty-five years, during which time I have been told to go in at least thirty-five different directions. Pastor, none of these have accomplished very much. We've seen surges in membership growth, but we've also seen people disappointed and leave. Is there one thing that is true for us forever?

IS THERE ONE THING THAT IS TRUE FOR US FOREVER?

Or does it change every time a new pastor comes? Is it really "new pastor" and "new vision"? Shouldn't there be one central vison for the church? Then one of the thoughtful asks, why does every pastor seem to have a different vison? Another asks, "What is it that defines us?" Where are we supposed to go? They have no desire to go through all of this again.

Faith-filled response

Most sincere believers recognize the danger of reading the Word of God through human eyes and not through the eyes of faith. Take Peter for example, he did walk on the water in the middle of the night, during a terrible storm. But when he saw the strong wind, he was afraid, and began to sink. He cried out, "Lord save me!" (See Mark 14:30). In other words, when he took his eyes off Jesus and on the wind and the waves, he began to sink. We must renew our minds! (see Romans 12:2).

It is possible for our minds to get in the way of our faith. We try to rationalize and intellectualize things and figure things out; which is often the opposite of a faith-filled response. What would have happened to many of the miracles in the Bible if the person God used from Moses to the apostle Paul, thought faith was optional?

STUDY GUIDE: CHAPTER 7 THE MINISTER AS SHEPHERD

1. The leadership model both authorized and demonstrated is the shepherd model. God rebuked the shepherds in Israel not for leading the flock away, but for not caring for the sheep.

2. The shepherd's problem was not poor leadership — but poor _____.

3. Paul's fear for the Corinthian church was that wholehearted devotion to Christ might be altered and a false Christianity might supplant the true faith.

4. False ministers had come into the church preaching a different Jesus.

5. The Holy Spirit with His power, gifts, and ministries have been replaced with traditions of men, legalism, and other external forms.

6. One pursuit that only the church can do is _____ _____ _____.

7. Most sincere believers recognize the danger of reading the Word of God through _____ _____.

SECTION TWO
FAITH THROUGH TRANSFORMATION

"Now faith is the assurance of things hoped for, the conviction of things not seen. For by it the people of old received their commendation. By faith we understand that the universe was created by the word of God, so that what is seen was not made out of things that are visible" (Hebrews 11:1-3 ESV).

CHAPTER EIGHT

MIXTURE OF LAW AND GRACE

*"For from His, fullness we have all received, grace upon grace.
For the law was given through Moses; grace and truth came
through Jesus Christ"* (John 1:16-17 ESV).

In the Scriptures, grace is constantly set in contrast to the Law of
Moses, God demanded righteousness from man; but under grace,
God in Christ gives righteousness to man. The law related to Moses
with *works*, but grace came by Jesus Christ – yes, *grace is Jesus Christ* –
and is yours by *faith. Faith is our positive response to God's grace.* The law
extended blessings to the good, but *grace* extends *salvation* to the bad!

Grace provides for us that which we do not deserve. The Bible
teaches grace as being of God and the gift of God to an undeserving
world, and God's grace is all-sufficient, but we must respond and
receive it by faith. The gospel believer is in Christ, *and "you are complete
in Him"* (Col. 2:10 NKJV).

Grace … In Christ Jesus

"You then, my child, be strengthened in the grace that is in Christ Jesus" (II Tim. 2:1 ESV).

All spiritual blessings are the result of grace, and grace is God's unmerited, unearned, undeserved favor toward humanity. There is absolutely nothing man or woman can do, give, or be in order to merit grace. Grace is bestowed upon gospel believers because of our faith in the finished work of Christ. Salvation is *all of grace,* without mixture. "But if it is by grace, then it is no longer based on works otherwise, grace would no longer be grace" (Romans 11:6 ESV). In fact, Hebrews 4 speaks of a "rest" in conjunction with faith. Faith only appropriates what God has already anticipated. Every need is already known and provided for, but not everybody responds to God.

Paul wanted these Christians to understand that they should be established with *grace,* not with the rituals of the law such as abstaining from meat or other practices. The heart of the gospel believer is all-sufficiency. There is nothing that can be added. God looks upon the heart, and when we serve Him with whole-hearted dedication we will eat right, drink right, and live right. Therefore, the Christian is established with grace – not with meats, drinks, observance of days, or rituals.

The likeness of Christ

Historically little has changed in the traditional Black Church for generations. Some of the rules have been modified and adapted to today's culture; and while some methods and strategies of doing church have changed a little, for the most part the core approach to reaching and discipling people is the same for many, many years. I joined the U.S. Army in 1958. I was asked at the processing station what my religious preference was. I told them I was Baptist. When I received my ID tags, my religious preference was listed as Protestant. Later, we found out that was the preference for all except those of the Catholic faith and the Jewish faith. Headstones of fallen soldiers were marked with the Cross or the Star of David. A little research revealed some 225 symbols are available today.

Church history records Martin Luther and John Calvin, two primary leaders of the Protestant Reformation, got it right concerning justification – how to be saved. "The righteous man shall live by faith" (Gal. 3:11 ESV). However, from the Reformation to this day, the church continues to struggle with sanctification or how one is transformed into the likeness of Jesus Christ. Like the Reformers, church leaders have drawn up rules some very ridged and others too lax, but not so clear as "You must be born again" in justification.

Many of their rules for sanctification are not closely related to Scripture. "Do the best you can with your behavior." God understands. Church Covenants, Constitutions, and by-laws are under constant revision in many cases due to compromising with the secular culture especially in the areas of sexuality and conformity. For example, when I read the church covenant as a young boy, members were told to abstain from the sale and use of alcoholic beverages. Today some churches have totally excluded that statement. But neither has the sale and use of drugs and paraphernalia been added.

Note the *mixture* of *law* and *grace* is taught and received by both conservatives and liberals today. The leaven of the law is even found in the presentation of the Gospel. In fact, almost all protestant churches are presenting a version of the Gospel leavened with the law. All of this equates to: "one is saved by grace through faith, but then for the rest of our earthly lives we do the best we can.' To be pleasing to God or "right" with God depends on my behavior – so I do my best to keep the rules here.

I am convinced most pastors and other church leaders do not have evil motives toward their people, but they are deceived and have believed the lie of the enemy that *behavior modification* is the goal God has set before them in ministry. Because helping people *control their flesh through human effort* and obedience to constitutions, by-laws, and other local church rules is not only a thankless and never-ending task, but most leaders also use any strategy that promises any measure of success. Guilt, shame, condemnation, conviction and even the use of God's name is used as a viable threat. So, when, I get to heaven; I will be fully sanctified." NO! NO! Sadly, this has been taught in many churches throughout the world for hundreds of years.

Many Christians are living in willful disobedience.

The teaching and practice of the above concepts are always teamed with sin; therefore, the true ministry of the Holy Spirit in the lives of believers is tremendously suppressed and limited. Satan hates the ministry of the Holy Spirit basically because the Holy Spirit is designated by Jesus Himself, *"But when He, the Spirit of truth, comes, He will guide you into all the truth"* (John 16:13 ESV). Furthermore, the Holy Spirit came "to convict the world of sin, righteousness, and judgment" (John 16:8 ESV).

His ministry is to guide us into all truth, and as we are convinced of the truth, we change our minds (repent) where we have believed a lie – and the truth sets us free. The Holy Spirit actively continues doing what He came to do in the world. The devil knows the *power of truth* has been unleashed in each true believer to be conformed to the image of Jesus and releases the Church to destroy the gates of hell.

The leaders of the Protestant Reformation were correct about Justification, [how one is saved]. Martin Luther discovered how one is saved *"The just shall live by faith"* (Gal. 3:11 KJV). That revelation changed the world. Afterward, he and John Calvin preached it. Both drew up rigid *rules of conduct*. This indicated that the individual was **"Saved by grace but perfected by a human effort."** Sermons hinged on so many, "do nots" that much of the preaching caused more harm than good. This approach over the centuries has produced a church that is judgmental, hopeless, helpless, fearful, ineffective, uninspired, and has standardized *spiritual immaturity or arrested spiritual development*. Most of it is a mixture of law and grace at best.

This malady of spiritual immaturity may be laid at the feet of pastors and other church leaders, who fear their people "growing up," because they may not be able to control them. They might develop minds of their own. They may begin to question the spiritual milk they are fed each week – even though much of it is religious gobble goop, starving people will eat whatever is put before them. Let me say, legalism [or other leaven], no matter the flavor leads to spiritual immaturity; but a revelation of grace and the finished work of Christ leads to spiritual maturity.

It is so tragic when sincere, pure-in-heart people attempt the impossible [legalism] repeatedly. Is there any wonder we have not impacted our culture; and today we have become the laughingstock to most casual observers – and we are deemed non-essential by our government and the world as noted in the present worldwide coronavirus epidemic.

I do not know about you, but after what we have been through, I am ready to see the church grow up and become the gates of hell demolisher, and love God with all her heart, the queen of battle – that Jesus is building.

Because a thing has not been practiced for two thousand years does not mean it is wrong. And likewise, because a thing has been practiced for two thousand years does not mean it is right. Remember, earlier we discussed the proverbial *mixture of law and grace.*

It seems that since the offerings of Cain and Abel there has been two standards for giving: 1) what God requires of us and, 2) what we are willing to give to God (see Gen. 4:1-5; Heb. 11:4). So, from the beginning we have had God's Word and humanities' estimates (substitutes). For example: "I am a sinner saved by grace." That is an unbiblical view of salvation, yet it is so widely received in the modern church. Church doctrine has been devastated by this leaven. However, over the centuries, this kind of legalistic leavened jargon has caused Christians to have a low view of salvation. It is seen in Evangelical, Denominational, Nondenominal, Reformed, Freewill, Holiness, or Charismatic and Pentecostals – the leaven of the law is found in even the most gracious preaching of the Gospel.

> If the devil could not keep you from being saved, his fallback strategy is to keep you in doubt that you are saved. If he failed to keep you from attempting to earn your salvation, he will try to deceive you into attempting to keep it through human effort. If he can no longer control your eternal destiny, he will try to fender you to be ineffective in your ability to influence others toward the glorious reality of union with Christ.[15]

A *new* thing

If you are a sinner, you have not been saved by grace. If you have been saved by grace you are not a sinner. In many of his letters to the churches, Paul addressed Christians as saints and never used the term "sinner" to identify believers. We were all born with a sin nature – the very reason we must be "born again"(see John 3:3).

---

[15] Clark Whitten, *Pure Grace* (Destiny Image Publishers, INC. 2012) 125

However, my new nature is not a sin nature. A person with a sin nature can only sin. A saint can be holy and sin, but not at the same time. All of us are *either* in Adam with a sin nature *or* in Christ with a new nature. Saints can sin, but that sin cannot undo the work of Christ and make a saint a sinner. When I was saved, I became the temple of the Holy Ghost and so did you!

I came into union with Christ. He had to create *a new person* who was a perfect dwelling place for His Spirit, which He did. I had to become *"a new creation"* (2 Cor. 5:17 ESV). I had to be "born again." Dead in my sins, I had to be raised to new life in Christ. God could not simply cover my sin as in the Old Covenant. He had to cleanse me of my sin. *"Though your sins are like scarlet, they shall be white as snow"* (Isaiah 1:18 ESV). David prays, *"Wash me thoroughly from my iniquity, and cleanse me from my sin"* (Psalm 51:2 ESV).

These two pictures from the Old Testament provide a preview of the forgiveness that ultimately comes through Christ in the New Testament. On occasion, Paul speaking to people who formerly lived sin saturated lives says, *"You were washed, you were sanctified, and you were justified in the name of the Lord Jesus Christ and by the Spirit of our God"* (1 Cor. 6:11 ESV). John writes, *"If we confess our sins, He is faithful and just to forgive us our sins and to cleanse us from all unrighteousness"* (1 John 1:9 ESV). Praise God! This cleansing is a gift from God, and not based on anything we have done – but altogether upon God's mercy. Paul says,

> *"But when the goodness and loving kindness of God our Savior appeared, He saved us, not because of works done by us in righteousness, but according to His own mercy, by the washing of regeneration and renewal of the Holy Spirit"* (Titus 3:4-5 ESV).

The clear message of the Bible is that there is nothing we can do to make our hearts clean before a holy God. We can work constantly, fervently pray, give abundantly, and love sacrificially – but our hearts will still be stained by sin.

By Faith Alone

Therefore, the Bible teaches that *faith alone in Christ alone is the only way to salvation from sin.*

- Faith is the realization that there is absolutely nothing you can do but *trust* in what has already been done for you in the life, death, and resurrection of Jesus Christ.
- Faith is the realization that God's pleasure in you will never be based upon your performance for Him.

Instead, God's pleasure in you will always be based upon Christ's performance for you. Come to Christ and He will cleanse your heart. Hear the truth of the gospel message. We do not have to work to wash away our sins as we turn from our sin to trust in the atoning work of Jesus Christ (see Gal. 3:10-14). *"The just shall live by faith"* (Gal. 3:11 NKJV).

Unsearchable riches of Christ

Peter described the "unsearchable riches of Christ"[16] as "the salvation" that Christ brought to us through His suffering and death on the cross. He said the prophets of the Old Testament saw this salvation afar off and called it **"the grace** that should come unto you."[17]

---

[16] 1 Peter 1:10

[17] Ibid.

They had heard **"from the spirit of Christ which was in them[18] and the glory that should follow."**[19] Notice, the grace that was seen by the prophets was also **"the glory"** that would come after Christ died and rose again. Of course, we believe the glory which should follow" was that which was **manifested** on the Day of Pentecost, however, it meant so much more than that. It is the "glory" of a **"New Creation"**[20] "created *in* Christ Jesus."[21]

God's eternal purpose

It is a *people* created in Christ that have never been seen *since* the day Adam *disobeyed God* and brought sin into the world.[22] This world or age began with the entrance of sin. Sin distorted God's image[23] into which Adam was created. So, in God's great plan of regeneration[24] beginning with a "new birth"[25] from above.

---

[18] 1 Peter 1:10

[19] Ibid.

[20] II Corinthians 5:17

[21] Ephesians 2:10

[22] *Aion,* "an age, a period of time, marked in the NT usage by spiritual or moral characteristics, is sometimes translated "world." In 1 Cor. 10:11, KJV. ESV "the end of the ages "probably signifying the fulfillment of the divine purposes concerning the ages regarding the sin and the church (see Rom. 16:25; 2 Tim. 1:9; Titus 1:2).

[23] God made man in His own "image," reflecting some of His own perfections: perfect in knowledge, righteousness, and holiness, and with dominion over the creatures (Gen. 1:26). Source: Vine's Complete Expository Dictionary of the Old and New Testament words (Thomas Nelson Publishers 1985) 244.

[24] Ibid. "Spiritual regeneration," Titus 3:5, involving the communication of a new life, the two operating powers to produce which are "the word of truth," James 1:18; 1 Peter 1:23, and the Holy Spirit, John 3:5, 6. Also see 2 Corinthians 5:17.

[25] Ibid. The new birth stresses the communication of spiritual life in contrast to

Three things about this new creation:

1. They are "free from sin" (see Romans 6:7, 18, 22).
2. They "abide in Christ" (John 15:5).
3. They "do not sin" (I John 3:5-6, 9).

God's grace is unlimited. Christ is grace. Christ is in the Christian and the Christian is in Christ. "Where sin abounded, *grace* abounded much more" (Romans 5:20 NKJV). The question of sin has been settled, once and for all through the one sacrifice of our Lord and Savior, Jesus Christ, who entered the holiest with His own blood and satisfied God by the offering of Himself. "So that as sin reigned in death even so grace might reign in righteousness to eternal life through Jesus Christ our Lord" (Romans 5:21 NKJV). Amen!

---

antecedent spiritual death John 3:3, 6.

STUDY GUIDE: CHAPTER 8 MIXTURE OF LAW AND GRACE

1. Grace provides for us that which we do not deserve. The Bible teaches grace as being of God and the gift of God to an undeserving world, and God's grace is all-sufficient, but we must respond and receive it by faith.

2. All spiritual blessings are the result of grace. "But if it is by grace, then it is no longer based on works: otherwise grace would no longer be grace" (Romans 11:6 ESV).

3. "The just shall live by faith" (Galatians 3:11 KJV) was preached by both Martin Luther and John Calvin. Both drew up rigid rules of conduct. This indicated that the individual was "saved by grace but perfected by human effort."

4. This approach over the centuries produced so many "do not" that much of the preaching caused more harm than good. It produced a church that is judgmental, hopeless, helpless, fearful, and ineffective. Mostly a mixture of law and grace.

5. Church doctrine has been devastated by this leaven. Over the centuries, this kind of legalistic leaven has caused Christians to have a low view of salvation.

6. The clear message of the Bible is that there is nothing we can do to make our hearts clean before a holy God. We can work constantly, fervently pray, give abundantly, and love sacrificially, but our hearts will still be stained by sin.

7. The question of sin has been settled, once and for all through the one sacrifice of our Lord and Savior, Jesus Christ.

CHAPTER NINE

"My little children, for whom I labor in birth again until Christ is formed in you. I would like to be present with you now and to change my tone; for I have doubts about you" (Galatians 4:19-20 NKJV).

One Sunday morning after one of my most successful (fishing trips) in the service. I landed a dozen new members. The question popped into my mind, "why should we bring a dozen new people into something that is not working?" That was the first time in thirty years of ministry that I had unmasked myself. I was convinced that the ministry I was leading was not working. It appeared to be working, but something was wrong All the formulas, strategies, mission statements, and visions – are not "making disciples." After several years of misery, I concluded, that when your preaching clashes with the environment (culture) – the environment wins.

Where was the *personal transformation?* We were engaged in a studied routine of religious activity *without change.* We were not seeing people coming to Christ in any great numbers. In fact, we were stuck in the same rut that so many churches found themselves when the COVID-19 hit. We were doing things right, but there was *little movement* from the Spirit. It was as though I was peering at an iceberg and knowing that what I saw was just the tip of the iceberg. I could see *transformation,* but the part of the iceberg underwater represents the church's infrastructure, customs, and traditions of the fathers – peoples' lives seemed to be the same throughout. It represents institutional church-based roles and hierarchy rather than a community rooted in relationships of love, obedience, and faith.

This leader model insists that the pastors should be CEO's or in house experts of church growth. Rather than, one who help people grow to mature disciples in Christ (shepherd model). During that period of my desperation God had been reshaping me. I had morphed in such a manner that I could never go back to the way I was. Jesus did not come so that we might live a life of institutional religion. He came so that we could receive new life *in Him* through supernatural regeneration and reconciliation. Institutional religion consists of believing certain truths and certain other things. As we saw while discussing different faiths, such superficial religion is running wild in the world today – and it was running wild in Jesus' day as well. We can take for example, Jesus's conversation with Nicodemus, a leader of the Jewish people. Nicodemus was like many professing Christians today; he possessed a measure of belief in and respect for Jesus while ordering his life around the commands of Scripture. He prayed, and he worshipped. He read and even taught the Bible. He lived a good moral life – all to honor God. On the outside everything was right, but on the inside, he had no supernatural spiritual life. This is the fallacy of institutional (superficial) religion: constantly striving to do impressive outward things apart from inward transformation. As we saw in another section, you will perpetuate the habit of practicing religion in the strength of the "flesh."

Paul confronted this problem within the Church in Galatian. He told them that their Christian life was begun in the Spirit by faith alone (v. 2; 2:16). Being made perfect by the flesh indicates that the Galatians were mistakenly trying to achieve perfection through *their own efforts,* especially through circumcision. This statement implies that the Galatian citizens had previously suffered for their faith, before they were tricked by the false gospel:

> *"O foolish Galatians! Who has bewitched you that you should not obey the truth before whose eyes Jesus Christ was clearly portrayed among you as crucified? This I only want to learn from you: Did you receive the Spirit by the works of the law, or by the hearing of faith? Are you so foolish? Have you suffered so many things in vain — if indeed it was in vain?"* (Gal. 3:1-4 NKJV).

The World's Greatest Need

All around the world today, people are equating the gospel of Jesus Christ with physical healing and material prosperity. Yes, Jesus is able to heal physical maladies, and yes, Jesus has authority over pain and diseases, but that is not the central message of the gospel of Christ. This is not the Good News of Christ, for the Good News is not primarily that Jesus will heal you of all your sicknesses and diseases right now — but that Jesus will ultimately forgive you of all your sins forever.

The good News of Christ is that if you have childlike faith in Jesus Christ, you will be reconciled to God for eternity.

Forgiveness is God's greatest gift because it meets our greatest need.

More than we need to be healed of cancer, we need to be cleansed of sin. More than receiving a heart transplant, we need our sins forgotten. And this is exactly what Jesus gives us in a *new heart*, cleansed of sin, that leaves us with nothing to fear.

A New Heart and a New Spirit

Many professing Christians believe that Jesus has cleansed them from their sins, yet there is no real change in their lives. However, this is not the way it supposed to be. In this section, I want to show you the *need* for the *indwelling power of the Holy Spirit*. And I must emphasize again that *no one* in his or her own strength is able to live *an overcoming life – free from sin's power and dominion*. He or she may grieve over their sins, shed a bucket of tears, but in their own willpower and ability neither can defeat their powerful and besetting sins.

The exile prophet Ezekiel preached *repentance* to the nation of Israel, he knew that God was grieved over Israel's backsliding and compromise. He told the people:

> *"Repent, and turn from all your transgressions, lest iniquity be your ruin. Cast away from you all the transgressions that you have committed, and make yourself a new heart and a new spirit ...... So, turn and live"* (Ezekiel 18:30-32 ESV).

In essence, he was telling them, "You know what you are doing is wrong, so why don't you stop it? Lay it down. Just say no to your besetting sin. Turn from it, be good, get yourself a new spirit and a new heart – "[both are beyond my ability to create]!" This is the heart of Jesus' call to follow Him. When we became Christians, we died, and Jesus became our life. Christ is alive in you, and the only way you can live is by faith in Him. Paul writes,

> "But if Christ is in you, although the body is dead because of sin, the Spirit is life because of righteousness. If the Spirit of Him who raised Jesus from the dead dwells in you, He who raised Christ Jesus from the dead will also give life to your mortal bodies through His Spirit who dwells in you" (Romans 8:10-11 ESV).

A believer can live according to the flesh with the result of death (see James 1:13-15), or else by the new spirit so, as to experience life in vv.7-11, Paul elaborates on these two possibilities, showing the possibility and the benefit of living according to the Spirit. Many churches who promote numbers and size cannot afford to preach and teach the truth about being *carnally minded* such as: to be carnally minded results in death v.6 – and that the *carnal mind* is an enemy of God. The mind of the flesh is hostile to God and can never submit itself to the law of God. Now having said that, there are many who think they are good enough in the "flesh" to go to heaven." In fact, in v.8, we are faced with another truth unknown to most: "being in the flesh" is different from "walking according to the flesh." Being in the flesh means being *unregenerate or sinful.* No one in this state can please God.

Christ died for sin once for all. He is now alive at the right hand of God. Since gospel believers have been joined to Christ and to His death and resurrection, they can now believe that they are alive to God.

Christians no longer live according to the flesh, under the control of their sinful human nature instead, with the Holy Spirit living in them and empowering them, they can live in a way pleasing to God. Give Him praises and glory.

STUDY GUIDE: CHAPTER 9 DISCIPLESHIP: IN AN ENVIORNMENT OF FAITH

1. Jesus came so we could receive new life in Him through _____ and _____.

2. Paul confronted this institutional religion which has a measure of belief in and respect for Jesus while ordering life around the commands of Scripture. He or she prays and worships, reads the Bible, and lives a good moral life, all to honor God. On the outside everything looks right, but on the inside there is no supernatural spiritual life. As we saw in another section, this person will perpetuate the habit of practicing religion in the strength of the "flesh." This is not the Good News of Christ. Again, no one can live an overcoming life free from sin in their own strength.

3. The good news of Christ is not primarily that Jesus will heal all your _____ and _____ right now, but Jesus will forgive you of all you sins forever.

4. Many professing Christians believe that Jesus has _____ them from their sins yet there is no real change in their lives.

5. We can see the need for the indwelling power of the Holy Spirit (see Romans 8:10-11).

6. We are faced with another truth unknown to most: "being in the flesh" is different from "walking according to the flesh." Being in the flesh means being unregenerate or sinful. No one in this state can please God. (v. 8).

7. It is so tragic when sincere, pure-in-heart people attempt the impossible [legalism] repeatedly. Is there any wonder why we have not impacted our culture; and today we have become the laughingstock to most casual observers.

CHAPTER TEN
THE LORD'S MULTIPLICATION (STRATEGY)

"And what you have heard from me in the presence of many witnesses entrust to faithful men, who will be able to teach others also" (II Timothy 2:2 ESV).

One of the most influential books in my personal library is a little booklet entitled "Born to Reproduce" by Dawson Trotman. From time to time, I like to go back and review some of the old pamphlets and leaflets of yesteryear. In just a few pages he makes the case that "every person who is born into God's family is to multiply." Yet he maintains that most Christians are not multiplying. He continues, "In every Christian audience, I am sure there are men and women who have been Christians for five, ten, or twenty years but who do not know of one person who is living for Jesus Christ today because of them."[26] This is a problem, Trotman says, and it's the reason the gospel has not yet spread to the nations today.

---

[26] Dawson Trotman, "Born to Reproduce," 5, 12. Retrieved from discipleship Library, http://www.discipleshiplibrary.com/pdfs/AA094.pdf.

In contrast, "the Gospel spread over the world during the first century without, television, internet, or printing press, because [the early church] produced [Christians] who were *reproducing.*" Trotman uses the illustration of how parents naturally reproduce children in the context of marriage to assert that, "every one of [God's] children ought to be a reproducer."[27] Similar to the married couple longing to see a natural birth, God has woven into the DNA of every Christian a desire to see a sinner supernaturally saved. So, it is reasonable to conclude that something is spiritually wrong at the core of any Christian's relationship with Christ that does not result in reproduction.

> Perhaps, it is reasonable to say, whenever you find a Christian who is not leading men and women to Christ – something is not right!

To be a disciple of Jesus then, is to make disciples of Jesus. Undoubtedly, this has been true ever since Jesus invited four men to follow Him. His words have echoed down through the centuries, and though denied, or ignored today; they are just as pertinent now as they were in the first century, when Jesus had commanded them.

Twenty-first Century Disciples

"Follow Me, and I will make you fishers of men" (Matt. 4:19 NKJV). These men whom Jesus *invited* to follow Him would spread the gospel all over the world. They would give their lives not simply to being disciples of Jesus, but *sacrificially* to making disciples of Jesus. And no matter what lies the devil-led legalists and false teachers are

---

[27] Ibid. 14, 10.

spreading today, God's design for twenty-first century disciples is precisely the same as the first century.

Jesus calls every one of His disciples to make disciples who makes disciples until the gospel penetrates every people group in the world!

Unite your life with Christ's life

When you come to Jesus all of life for the disciple becomes a faith walk 24/7. Everything that belongs to Him now belongs to you. As stated earlier:

- His righteousness becomes yours.
- His Spirit fills your spirit.
- His love becomes you love.
- His mind becomes your mind.
- His desires become your desires.
- His will becomes your will.
- His purpose becomes your purpose.
- His power becomes your power.

This reality in the disciple's life marks the difference between the false shallow, religious experience of most Christians and supernatural *regeneration* through which the Christian life becomes the *outliving* of the *indwelling* Christ. For the Christian, this biblical truth is not open for debate, discussion, or unbelief. This is a life that involves an authentic Bible-based Christian life that has experienced an awakening [*made alive*] by the Spirit, truth, love, passion, purpose, and power of Jesus Christ. This is what Jesus means in the words, "Follow Me." As

Jesus walked along the shore, he told these fishermen. "Follow Me, and *I will make you* fishers of men" (Matthew 4:19 ESV).

There is a great lesson in this passage for the church today. Notice in His invitation, Jesus does not tell His disciples what He will *call* them to do. Instead – He tells them what He will *cause* them to do. Again, the commands He would give to them could only be accomplished by – the work that *He would do in them*. This next statement is important: as these disciples followed Jesus, He *transformed* everything about their lives:

- Their thoughts
- Their desires
- Their will
- Their relationships

Ultimately the very purpose for which they lived – as a result of being disciples of Jesus, every one of them actually gave their lives not for being disciples of Jesus, but sacrificially to making disciples of Jesus.

The fruit of transformation

We see the fruit of transformation in these disciples was *multiplication* through their disciple-making. As Jesus transformed the disciples, they grew eager to proclaim the gospel; which changed their purpose for living. Ten out of eleven of Christ's Apostles were martyred sacrificially because they went into the world committed to making disciples. And Jesus came and said to them, "All authority in heaven and on earth has been given to me:

> *"Go therefore and make disciples of all nations, baptizing them in the name of the Father and of the Son and of the Holy Spirit, teaching them to observe all that I have*

commanded you. And behold, "I am with you always, to the end of the age" (Matthew 28:18-20 ESV).

If you have heard anyone teach this scripture before, you probably know the phrase "Therefore, go" is more closely translated to mean "As you are going." It implies *action*. The word go literally means "travel" or "journey." Jesus' instructions assume that we will *continue* this apprenticeship model He taught. We become more proficient as we travel through different environments along our journey.

Observing the church today, it seems we have forgotten the command of Christ to go, baptize, and teach all nations; just as if it has been rescinded. Biblically, from the very beginning of Christianity, we know that every single disciple of Jesus Christ is intended to make disciples. Like the early disciples, we are supernaturally empowered to be fishers of men. Not even *death* could stop them from obeying this command. Many Churches corporately and Christians individually are living in willful disobedience mainly due to the lack of biblical teaching and application. So, what is keeping us from obeying this Kingdom command today?

The purpose of the Spirit in Discipleship

In both the Old and the New Testament, the filling of the Spirit in God's people is clearly linked to a particular purpose: the verbal proclamation of God's Word and the ultimate accomplishment of His will. This is exactly what we see Jesus accomplishing through His Church in the New Testament. Though Jesus has ascended to heaven (see Acts 1), He continues to work. Jesus pours out His Spirit in power upon His people.

Why don't they listen?

Despite all the above. People still cry "I just want to be a Christian. I don't want to be a disciple." "I like my life the way it is." "I believe that Jesus died for my sins, and I will see Him when I die." "Why do I have to be a disciple?" "You don't have to be a disciple to go to heaven." Many of you who are reading this will agree with one or more of such conclusions. However, the answer you give reveals the gospel you believe and the way you live. Though the truth of the question is biblically presented, a growing majority of Christians are willing only to give what is convenient for them. The challenge we face today in much of today's preaching and teaching is:

- A faith that does not transform.
- A Christianity that is not biblical.
- Willful disobedience.
- Non disciples teaching disciples with more than 50% dropping out.
- A mixture of law and grace.
- Truth mixed with leaven.
- A test for salvation that is doctrinal rather than behavioral.
- Ritualized evangelism
- A commitment to Christ without a commitment to the church.

We have made it so easy and convenient to enter the Christian life by skipping the repentance commitment and regeneration that provide the power to live a holy Christian life.

STUDY GUIDE: CHAPTER 10

1. There are people who have been Christians 5, 10, or 20 years but do not know one person who is saved _____ of them.

2. To be a disciple of Jesus then is to make _____ of Jesus.

3. When you come _____ _____ all of _____ for the disciple become a faith walk.

4. In Jesus' command to, "Follow Me" (Matthew 4:19), He does not tell His disciples what He will _____ them to do, but He tells them what He will _____ them to do.

5. The filling of the Spirit in God's people is clearly linked to the verbal proclamation of God's Word and the ultimate _____ of His will.

6. Much of the church today are living in willful _____ due mainly to a lack of biblical teaching and _____.

7. We have made it so easy and convenient to enter the Christian life by skipping the _____ commitment and _____ that provide the power to live a holy Christian life.

CHAPTER ELEVEN
THE NEW REALITIES FACING THE LOCAL CHURCH

"The sons of Issachar who had understanding of the times, to know what Israel ought to do" (1 Chronicles 12:32 NKJV).

Many of the committed Christians who [though few] still faithfully occupy the family pews and hold on to the nostalgic hope that tomorrow will be yesterday. Others want their churches to catch up with the times and meet the challenges of the present generation – but they don't know how. And still others fight the inevitable changes for the sake of some traditions that would no doubt be better off abandoned.

Likewise, a large number of para-church ministries are starting to show signs of aging. Many of the founders are gone; many will go within the next couple of decades. And many of the rising generation of leaders, who often seem to lack the vision of the founders, are accused of merely managing other's dreams. What is happening in our churches and our para – ministries? And what can we do about it? Many saved and some unsaved people desperately want to know. What is happening? **CHANGE!** Dramatic, difficult, but necessary change!

Change is unavoidable

Change is inevitable – part of life. Without change life would soon become an intolerable drudgery. We welcome new experiences, variety in foods, the coming of the four seasons, and answered prayers. When the status quo becomes unbearable, we do everything we can to initiate change.

At the same time, we hate the changes brought about by COVID-19, fires in the west, hurricanes, civil unrest, social upheavals, and intrusions into our comfort zones. Change would be troubling enough if every one of us were isolated and unconnected from everyone else. Then, again the coronavirus upset everything and everybody as change came to all at the same time, globally. What happens to individuals and families also happens to groups and individuals. While the group changes as a result of the members – but the corporate can also control changes in the individuals.

In other words, we cannot do our changing alone or assume that others will wait for us to catch up. Everyone is moving. Each member of the church is changing while the society is changing. Change is not a choice. How we handle change is. By the end of the twentieth century, the currents of society became more powerful and closer. The rapid changes brought on by drugs, murders, violence, environmental pollution, political polarization, and economics made it difficult for any individual, family, business, church, or community to not be affected. No matter where we stand on the issues, change is inevitable.

We hear much speculation concerning where God is in all of this? If everything changes, does God also change? The Bible teaches two theological truths concerning God's relationship to change:

1. God is immutable, meaning He is changeless. God is above and beyond our finite human changes. His standards are absolute. God is the *one* fixed point in *all* that is in motion in our lives.

2. God is also sovereign. He orders and accomplishes His will in human affairs. He is deeply involved in the circumstances of our lives.

Though the odds are greatly against it, most people treat their circumstances in life as matters of chance. However, as Christians we believe that God works in and through *change* to accomplish His purposes. What may seem senseless to us fits perfectly into His plan.

Barriers to Change

Although all institutions have a natural tendency to change, it seems the church experiences for more barriers to change than most others. Some resistance is necessary for the good, otherwise they would be turned and twisted with every wind and doctrine that blows through. Unfortunately, resistance to change can create these barriers. Unless they are removed or overcome, the God-given missions are threatened.

1. *Institution over purpose*

    In the beginning most churches are purpose driven, even if they don't have a purpose statement. They establish a place of worship for a certain group of people or a denomination. After a generation the purpose is either *fulfilled* or *forgotten*. However, the building, budget, and members are still there. Now the purpose subtly changes to "keeping the institution" going. Institutional focus is one of the *primary* enemies of change because change will alter the institution's way of doing things (the status quo). Soon the institution faces threats, which normally puts the church board on the defense and "resistance to change" sets in. Unconsciously even newcomers become a threat.

Only when institutional death is imminent, the holdouts may be willing to change – but often too late. Although, many traditional churches are essentially judgmental toward the lost secular people outside, they seem to be motivated by the need for new members to stop their stagnation and decline, or to pay the bills, or to maintain the institutional church.

2. *While the church was sleeping*

I came across an illustration one day concerning coca cola. The inquiry was made that coca cola is known about, drank, and loved all over the world. So, why spend the vast amount of the budget on advertisements about a product so widely known? The advertising department defended their budget with the following statement: "Everyday millions of people die who knew about coca cola; and everyday millions of people are born who never heard of coca cola."

We've heard the adage (or fact) that the gospel is only one generation from extinction. Everyday millions of people die who have heard the gospel, and every day millions are born who have never heard the gospel! Does that explain, the many warnings, rebukes, and strong encouragements we find in the pages of Scripture? Because God knows human nature and the heart of man. It is easy to let up, and get comfortable, become distracted or busy *(about the wrong thing)*, pursue leisure, love this world, and *slowly* fall.

Much of what people are hearing from many of our preachers and teachers is about God's blessings and grace. It seems we have been sold on a Christian life as a walk in the park when in reality, it is a walk on a battlefield.

Conforming to the world and allowing our faith to erode to lukewarm status happens over many years. Sadly, when this occurs, we are not much concerned about spiritual things – let alone obedience to God. We can still be saved – but our witnessing and disciple-making abilities are dulled, ineffective or unproductive. We must be diligent, set apart unto Christ, and intentional about living for the Lord. Jesus taught His disciples about the challenge of seeking temporary things and losing sight of the kingdom of God. God has preserved America these many years with peace and prosperity [through obedience] (see Duet. 28:1-14). But we have forgotten God. It behooves each of us then, to humble ourselves before our offended Creator, to repent and confess our individual and national sins, and pray for forgiveness. Today we are witnessing an even greater shift in the polarization of national, state, and local politics, open immorality, vicious crimes, sickness, and diseases in this country revealing the heart of mankind [through disobedience] (see Duet. 28:15-68):

> *Woe to those who call evil good*
> *and good evil,*
> *who put darkness for light,*
> *and light for darkness,*
> *who put bitter for sweet?*
> *and sweet for bitter!*
> Isaiah 5:20 ESV

Do you agree that in the rebellion against God today, sin is being openly promoted? Where have all the shepherds gone? Where are the warning voices of the shepherds and the *essential* church? Sleeping? Yes, we are surrounded by evil. There is a war on *truth*, even in the church. Through *compromising with evil,* our nation's moral and spiritual foundations have been slackened, culture is collapsing, and our defenses need to be reinforced.

Do not be overcome by evil – but overcome evil with good (Isaiah 12:21 ESV). Amen!

STUDY GUIDE: CHAPTER 11 THE NEW REALITIES FACING THE LOCAL CHURCH

1. Some Christians fight inevitable changes for the sake of some _____ that would be better off to abandon.

2. Though change is not a choice – how we _____ it is.

3. The Bible teaches two theological truths concerning God's relationship to change: 1) God is immutable, which means He _____ _____. 2) God is sovereign, which means He _____ and _____ His will in human affairs.

4. Today we are witnessing an even greater shift in the polarization of national, state, and local politics, open immorality, vicious crimes, conformity in the church culture, sickness, diseases, and curses (see Duet. 28:15-68).

5. Where are the _____ voices of the _____ and the _____ church?

6. Sin is being _____ promoted today through an open war against truth, even in the _____.

7. Through compromising with evil, or nation's moral and spiritual foundations have been shaken to their core, culture is collapsing, and our defenses need to be reinforced (see Isaiah 5:20, 12:21).

CHAPTER TWELVE
ONE VINE (JESUS)

"I am the vine, you are the branches, He who abides in Me, and I in him, bears much fruit; for without Me you can do nothing" (John 15:5 NKJV).

"Therefore, say to them, "Thus declares the LORD of hosts, "return to me," says the LORD of hosts, and I will return to you, says the LORD of hosts" (Zechariah 1:3 ESV).

In March of 1863, President Abraham Lincoln, with full agreement of the U.S. Senate, declared a national day of fasting and prayer to God. This was only eighty-seven years after celebrating America's independence and two years before the end of the Civil War, Lincoln was concerned about the country's *pride, financial blessings, and comfort,* which go hand in hand with *spiritual apathy.* Part of his national proclamation and call to *repentance* stated:

"We know that, by His divine law, nations like individuals are subjected to punishments and chastisements in the world; ...We have been the recipients of the choicest bounties of Heaven. We have been preserved, these many years, in peace and prosperity. We have grown in numbers, wealth, and power ... But we have forgotten God."

"We have forgotten the gracious hand which preserved us in peace; ... and we vainly imagined, in the deceitfulness of our hearts, were produced by some superior wisdom and virtue of our own. Intoxicated with unbroken success, we have become too self-sufficient to feel the necessity of redeeming and preserving grace, too proud to pray to the God that made us! It Behooves us then, to humble ourselves before the offended Power, to confess our national sins, and to pray for forgiveness."[28]

Throughout the Scriptures we find verses of warning quite relevant and appropriate for revealing the present-day heart of mankind and the evil shift in morality today. America like old Israel has done evil in the sight of the Lord, and served other gods, such as self, money, pleasure, politics, immorality, and they have forsaken the Lord God.

I am sure you will readily agree that in the evil rebellion against God today, sin is being *openly promoted*. Where is the voice of warning coming from the essential church today? Time is moving, waiting for no one. So, what do we do? We look to the timeless principles in the Word of God!

"Therefore, say to them, "Thus declares the LORD of hosts, "Return to Me," says the LORD of hosts, "and I will return to you, says the LORD of hosts "(Zechariah 1:3 ESV).

---

[28] Abraham Lincoln, "Proclamation Appointing a National Fast Day," Abraham Lincoln Outline, 3.30.1863, http://www.abrahamlincolnonline.org/lincolnline.org/Lincoln/speeches/fast.htm

The essential church

In His eternal plan God has always intended having a people of His own in whom He can take pleasure and dwell among. The chief goal of God in the creation of man was to have a people of whom He could say, "I am theirs and they are mine." Of course, God's plan included more than the average individual's view of church-going and attending "a place of worship." It speaks of a community whose center of gravity is God in Christ and above all else – they belong to Him.

Perhaps the nearest that the world has ever seen was the glorious New Testament church described in Acts 2-4 *"where they were together,"* not simply together for an hour on Sunday morning but knitted and built together, a part of Jerusalem's society but still somehow apart from it. Not just anybody could belong or be associated with them without like-minded purpose. Unlike many of our local churches today, where we say, "whosoever will come," for many that's all the welcome includes, just "come!"

Today numbers and size are more important and above all else simply to keep the institution going. Such priority-setting has been abandoned during the coronavirus epidemic because, it seems that the weak and the unsaved (faction) of the institutional attendance has learned to survive despite closed doors. Again, we find ourselves at the mercy of philosophy, science, and reason (earthly wisdom).

It's like sticking your forefinger into a pail of water then pulling it out. Immediately, the space your finger occupied was filled with water, no matter how long you held it there, the results are always the same. The hole your finger made disappears instantly and yes; the whole pail of water remains.

One Nation

As a nation, we have at times, made military alliances which allowed some of our troops to come directly under the command of foreign military leaders. In order to make it work our troops must be secularized by taking God and Christianity out of the Chain of Command. As I stated in an earlier section, America's scientists are not the only group with a high number of atheists at (70%), but sadly, there is also a large presence of atheists, secularists, and non-affiliates in the U.S. Armed Forces.

Atheists, secularists, and extreme progressives and extreme rightists want no God or His people interfering with their agenda. In fact, they are at every level of education and throughout the other institutions of our society. Just today it was announced that Greg Epstein, has been named president or chief of the chaplains for the religious community at Harvard University.[29] He has served as Harvard's humanist chaplain since 2005.

At the same time a biblical worldview and Christianity have been reduced to matters of mere speculation for many. The traditional model of marriage, and biblical counseling for the family are antiquated in our post-modern society. Today, people create their own model of morality. I would venture to say, we are now producing more atheists not only in our schools, and homes, but also in our churches. God forbid!

As we described earlier, the reputations of Christians are not always perfect. Eighty-four per cent say they personally know a Christian; but just fifteen per cent say their lifestyles are noticeably more positive than the norm. Recent polls show that those claiming to be Christians has decreased by twelve percent since the outset of COVID-19. For too many high profiled people abandon the family,

---

[29] Assessed 9/26/21 by Stephen M. Lepore for Dailymail.Com MailOnline logo.

objective truth, moral accountability, and the sacredness of life and human rights. Sadly, elected officials, public educators, and celebrities endlessly talk about the sacredness of life and human rights – but virtually always from a perspective of moral relativism.

Daily we see and hear, "It is my right to marry whomever I choose," or "It is my right to define my gender for myself," or "It is my right to have an abortion." These "rights" are assumed and acted upon. However, meaningful discussions to the contrary are rarely allowed.

These varied opinions just skate along the surface of how far America has strayed away from God and the Word of God. Even at our best living, sin still lie at our doors today, we just step over it and self-righteously keep stepping. If not careful, we will leave another generation of young people drowning in our selfish ambitions toward the material and extreme hypocrisy concerning the spiritual. One day at a store, my wife asked the cashier why the prices there were higher than at the larger retailers. The salesperson answered, that's why we are called "convenient stores" because we are "convenient" – they are found in some of the most unlikely locations "for your convenience." There are many lies embedded in church culture that we even as church folk buy into for convenience.

As I stated in an earlier section, *individualism* is more widespread here in America than other parts of the world, because in individualistic societies the "self" is king. Society has set some "silent issues" that are pure sin-based, and everybody know it. But for the sake of self, "that's just the way it is." This selfishness based on (individualism) can consume a whole people, a whole society, a whole church, a whole denomination, or a whole nation as we see happening in America today.

> We will not adjust the Bible to the age, but we will
> adjust the age to the Bible! Charles Spurgeon

The devil has made inroads into the American church through secularism (no God) which we all have seen grow generation after generation enveloping whole segments of our population into secular solutions for example, we have public school systems all over this nation, but "for the convenience" of the affluent, a system of private schools has been established transferring those resources from the public school system. Sadly, our government at all levels have become the spearhead for separation from a biblical worldview to a secular worldview even in our churches.

In His Presence

Younger generations are craving the presence and power of the Holy Spirit. A spike in spiritism and other cultic religious groups is an indictment to the church today. As I mentioned in other sections of this book, people, young and old are leaving the church to discover *a* spiritual experience. What a tragedy! Let's let this generation know, *those who are of the faith [Jews and Gentiles] are spiritual sons and daughters of Abraham.* If the apostle Paul was here to react to that, I imagine he would say, "as I inquired of the Galatians, "Are you so foolish? Having begun in the Spirit, are you now being perfected by the flesh?"(see Galatian 3:3). Undoubtedly, the Galatians were *mistakenly* trying to achieve perfection through their own efforts, especially through circumcision. Praise God! In this season, churches and para ministries are rising out of this institutional false gospel by the power of the Holy Spirit, who is our Teacher. They are no longer satisfied with spring showers; the churches are longing for:

- The deluge (see Haggai 2:9).
- The river to flow (Ezekiel 47).
- They will not quench the Holy Spirit (1 Thessalonians 5:19).
- They will not grieve the Holy Spirit (Ephesians 4:30).
- They will minister to the Lord (Isaiah 56:6).

The presence of God yields many unimaginable outcomes. A survey of the gospels reveals an intrinsic connection between God's presence and the expulsion of demonic activity (see Mark 1:39). Recently, our church saw a demonized person set free and saved. At the beginning of the 21st century churches were infatuated with novel technology, innovative service openers in some cases pyrotechnics, to praise dancers, and other attractional elements to reach people. A genuine attempt to reach those on the outside has led to neglect of "prayer and Word ministries" for all people (see Isaiah 56:7).

I do thank God for the Spirit-filled, blood washed spiritual remnant in this country, who have not compromised nor bowed to Baal. With all the ills that we are going through – we are still one nation! There are many diabolical segments in this country that think America needs a makeover (non-spiritual). Don't give up saints! Pray, pray and let us pray with clean hands lifted up to a holy God. The Hebrew verb translated *pray* in God's promise concerns the revival of Israel. It can also mean "to intervene," or to "arbitrate."

> *"If My people who are called by My name will humble themselves, and pray and seek My face, and turn from their wicked ways, then I will hear heaven, and will forgive their sin and heal their land"* (2 Chronicles 7:14 KJV).

If God's people would do three things, God would respond in three ways. The Lord's people needed to become **humble,** that is, confess their sin; they needed to **pray** and repent; and they needed to **turn,** or come back to Him. If they did, God promised He would **hear, forgive** and **heal** them (the land!).

The charge to our spiritual leaders concerning that time is the unintentional robbing younger generations of a true encounter with God; which actually led to a "driving away" rather than their "drawing in."

If we are going to rally the younger generations, we need to lay aside the trinkets of man and yield to the pure "power of the gospel" (see Romans 1:16) for organic spread of God's presence, power, and ministry of the Holy Spirit. As the Christian lives by faith, God continues to save him or her from the power of sin to live righteously. Let's begin with two verses in Romans 5:5 and 8:9:

> *"Now hope does not disappoint, because the love of God has been poured out in our hearts by the Holy Spirit who was given to us"* (Romans 5:5 NKJV).

Perseverance produces character. As Christians endure trials and tribulations, and certainly there are enough to go around, God works in them to develop certain qualities and virtues that will strengthen them and draw them closer to Him. The results is **fortified hope** in God and His promises.

This hope that Christians have of their future glory with God will not disappoint them by being unfulfilled. Certainly, they will not suffer shame or humiliation because of their hope. Why? Because the Christian can be confident that the love of God has been poured out. Praise God! He loved us while we were without strength and ungodly. In some of my writings, I use the term saints, disciples, Christ-followers or believers.

In this book I stress the word (Christian), because its high time that we come to terms with the truth that God holds each of us responsible for the souls of some unsaved people that we walk by every day. We have the same access to God the Father, God the Son, and God the Holy Spirit. We have the same biblical truths (Bible), and commands from our Lord and Savior, Jesus Christ. It was the Christians that "turned the world upside-down," "the Christians who were fed to lions, burned alive, and sawed asunder." Many became as beggars because of their faith, they were deemed unemployable (refusing to make their idols or bow to Caesar); which **fortified their obedience.** They are our examples and witnesses to every generation of what the Lord requires of us (see Hebrews 11), we call that chapter, "the Hall of Faith." We will realize that God uses our trials to prunes us into fruitful vessels (branches) through whom He can bless the world. Like many true Christians who have gone before us, Not only the trials and tribulations pruned and shaped their Christian life (character) but they also **fortified their faith.** The Bible tells us, "the just (justified) shall walk by faith"

God loves us just the way we are – but He loves us too much to leave us the way we are (see John 15:16; Philippians 1:6).

He loved us so much, He sent His Son to die for us (see v. 8). This next statement is very important. **The moment a person trusts in Christ, he or she receives the Holy Spirit who constantly encourages them in their hope in God.** Please note the second verse is a follow up: *"If anyone does not have the Holy Spirit, he or she is not one of His"* (Romans 8:9 NKJV). Christians no longer live-according to the *flesh,* under the control of their sinful human nature. Instead, with the Spirit living inside them and empowering them, they can live in a way pleasing to God.

STUDY GUIDE: CHAPTER 12 ONE VINE (JESUS)

1. We know that by His _____ _____, nations like individuals are subjected to punishments and chastisements in the _____.

2. In the evil rebellion against God today, _____ is being openly _____.

3. Recent polls show that those who claim to be a Christian in America has been reduced by _____%.

4. _____ is more widespread in here in America than any other _____ _____ _____ _____.

5. The presence of God _____ many unimaginable outcomes.

6. God promised His people, if they would _____ themselves, _____ and _____, then He would hear, _____ and _____, _____.

7. If anyone does not have the _____ of Christ, he is not His.

CHAPTER THIRTEEN
WHO ARE WE BECOMING?

"And you shall love the Lord your God with all your heart and with all your soul and with all your mind and with all your strength. The second is this: "You shall love your neighbor as yourself" (Mark 12:30-31 ESV).

Through the unfolding timeline of Scripture, we see God in relationship with a new people. A group of people *called* together for His purpose. In most of the New Testament letters written to the earliest generation of Christians, as they were struggling to understand their calling as the people of God, the *"you"* Paul, James, and Peter wrote about are not singular – but plural?

For better or for worse in season or out of season, both exist even in the best churches. Christians are called into community to be God's people. Jesus said the Greatest Commandment is two commandments to love God and to love others (see Matthew 22:36-40; Luke 10:17; Mark 12:30-31). It is voluntary disobedience if we agree and then act only on part 1 and disregard the 2nd part.

The pandemic has caused the church to reexamine the way she serves the community of believers. Many pastors have felt the pain in the weeks that followed an extended period of closure due to reduced attendance, offerings, and gathering times. Some leaders have suggested closing the doors of their church for good, as they pursue other professions (due to low finances). As I have stated in another section, others have returned with fewer people to go deeper and come back stronger. God reminds us that He is the Rock, and if we build His church on His Word – we will make it.

Our highest calling is love for God and others.

Participating in whatever capacity in the life of the church requires us to practice this great love. Church enables us to regularly come together to express our love to God in worship. And we are given endless opportunities to love others – and be loved by others. Some of the people outside the church can see the value of church, but *two* hindrances keep them from deep participation:

1. They sense that God's presence is absent from the church.
2. They suspect that Christians are really missing the point.

Why are we here?

We are here because the church should be the place where we can experience God's presence in the community of His people. Despite all the stellar programming and pyrotechnics employed in churches today; the one thing people are seeking is a powerful encounter with the living God. Many leave still seeking. Certainly, a person must be attuned to the Spirit of God in order to sense His presence.

Many people who are visiting the church service can overcome the obstacles because they are spiritually seeking to tune in to the Spirit. Again, some leave disappointed. When all is said and done, churchless and churched people realize that the main event is yet to come. They come to meet God. Most people have other places to gather with people they don't know for personal enrichment. But a local body of believers is the only place one can meet God together with *His* people!

Jesus or Pharisee

One of the common conclusions confronting present-day Christianity is that it is a religion over-ladened with hypocrites. Barna researchers' findings reveal:

- That most self-identified Christians in this country are characterized as (self-righteous) by having the attitudes and actions they identified as Pharisaical (51%).

- That one out of seven or 14% of today's self-identified Christians seem to represent actions and attitudes consistent with those of Jesus.

- That some have a mix of action and attitude. About one-fifth of Christians are Christlike in attitude, but often represent pharisaical actions (21%). Another 14% of respondents tend to be defined as Christ-like in actions but motivated by self-righteous hypocritical attitudes.[30]

True Righteousness is of God

True righteousness is of God, any other righteousness is counterfeit. As mentioned in an earlier section, there are two

---

[30] Accessed 8/28/21 (https://discipling101.files.wordpress.com/2014/06/jesus-or-pharisee-graphic-02.jpg.

approaches to receiving the righteousness of God. One common approach is to try to earn righteousness or right standing with God is through *performance*. That is what the nation of Israel tried to do. The Scripture says, *But Israel, which followed the law of righteousness, hath not attained to the law of* righteousness. That approach will *always fail. Why?* Because we fail.

We might do better or look better than someone else in the moment, *"but all of us have sinned and come short of the glory of God"* (Romans 3:23). Thus, the only approach to righteousness that works is that we must receive it as a gift *of faith* (see Ephesians 2:8-9).

Why is it that a person who is seeking so hard to please God can be rejected, while a person who has not sought God at all can come into a righteous relationship with Him?

Paul answered his own question. The answer is *faith* and *its object*. This is one of the most important doctrinal questions in Scripture. Like with many of us, the Jews were zealous toward the things of God – but their faith was in themselves (see Romans 10:2).

They thought they could earn God's favor by their acts of righteousness.[31] By the same token, the Gentiles had no holiness to trust in. So, when the Gentiles heard the Gospel that Jesus paid man's debt – they readily accepted His "gift" of salvation, while the religious Jews could not give up their trust in themselves for salvation. The same problem exists today.

---

[31] Israel had a real zeal for God outwardly, they were very religious. But their efforts were not according to knowledge. Like so many today, they lacked a correct understanding of the kind of worship God wanted from them.
God's righteousness belongs to God, and it is that righteousness God gives to those who trust Christ for salvation.

Millions of Christians are trying to live holy lives, but they don't have *true* faith in Jesus as their Savior. If these people had to stand before the Lord today and He asked them what they had done to deserve salvation, they would immediately start giving Him all their acts of holiness: church attendance, financial giving, committee meetings, and volunteerism, etc. In His Word, God has revealed to people how they should live, but no matter how their actions are compared to other people they always miss the perfect standard of God. No one can live up to God's perfect way in their own efforts (strength). We *all* fall short of His glory (see Romans 3:23).

Being wise like the world

Today our university and seminary professors are proud of their degrees from the leading liberal and progressive universities. It's amazing how the early church turned the world upside down led by such men as Peter and John, whom the Bible says were "unlearned and ignorant men" (Acts 4:13 KJV). In the early days of the Pentecostal Movement the churches were not sophisticated. The movement came out of the Azusa Street Revival[32] which took place in a converted barn. The principal leader in that outpouring was a humble black preacher from Texas named William Seymour. For further study on this worldwide movement see my book, *"Is There Not a Cause?"*[33] I'm all for a solid education as a tool – but not as a replacement for the Holy Spirit's power, gifts, and ministries. In an earlier section, Paul asked the Galatians a penetrating question, which should be revived in all our churches today: *"Are you so foolish? Having begun in the Spirit are you now made perfect by the flesh?"* (Galatians 3:3 KJV).

---

[32] Jay R. Leach, *Is There not a Cause?* (Trafford Publishing, 2017) 33-34

[33] Ibid.

In context, Paul was referring to relying on the *works of the Law to be saved*, as if you could be saved by grace through faith but only reaching your spiritual goal of sanctification by getting circumcised according to the Law. Paul made it clear, this was another gospel (see Galatians 1:6-10). As the New Living Translation Paraphrases:

"How foolish can you be? After starting your new lives in the Spirit, why are you now trying to become perfect by your own human efforts?" NLT

Sold Out

Two thousand years ago Jesus died on the cross, rose from the grave on the third day, ascended to the right hand of God the Father Almighty, afterward He sent the Holy Spirit to establish His church. Since those days so long ago, there have been rapid, radical, sweeping, and revolutionary changes. Daily we are seeing changes in institutions, morals, secular, and church cultures that were unimaginable two or three generations ago. These changes are leading many people to believe that God is now forced by them to alter or modify His plans for the church and humanity as well. Not only are we witnessing a great "falling away" as the Bible has stated would happen – but more astonishing is that great "falling away from the truth" to believe the "big lie!"

The Big Lie

The Scripture tells us, *"For what can be known about God is plain to them, because God has shown it to them. For his invisible attributes namely, his eternal power and divine nature, have been clearly perceived, ever since the creation of the world, in the things that have been made. So, they are without excuse. For although:*

- *they knew God*
- *they did not honor him as God*
- *they did not give thanks to him*
- *they became futile in their thinking*
- *their foolish hearts were darkened.*
- *Claiming to be wise, they became fools,*
- *they exchanged the glory of the immortal God for images resembling mortal man and birds and animals and creeping things.*

*Therefore, God gave them up in the lusts of their hearts to impurity, to the dishonoring of their bodies among themselves, **because they exchanged the truth about God for a lie** and worshiped and served the creature rather than the Creator, who is blessed forever! Amen.*

For this reason God gave them up to dishonorable passions. For their women exchanged natural relations for those that are contrary to nature; and men likewise gave up natural relations with women and were consumed with passions for one another, men committing shameless acts with men and receiving in themselves the due penalty for their error.

And since they did not see fit to acknowledge God, God gave them up to a debased mind to do what ought not to be done. They were filled with all manner of unrighteousness, evil, covetousness, malice. They are full of envy, murder, strife, deceit, maliciousness. They are gossips, slanders, haters of God, insolent, haughty, boastful, inventors of evil, disobedient to parents, foolish, faithless, heartless, ruthless. Though they know God's righteous decree that those who practice such things deserve to die, they not only do them but give approval to those who practice them.

Probably, most Christians would agree if asked, whether we need a restoration of the faith to a belief in the truth. However, I believe most people today if asked the question, "Has God been forced to change

140

his plans for humankind?" While they probably would not have the nerve to say, yes" (see Romans 1:21-23); but they continue to act it out, this goes on gradually until they are completely brainwashed. The outcome is these people believe that the Bible must be updated in line with new developments. Have you joined the crowd, who believe the following?

- We are to believe the Bible must be reinterpreted to coincide with contemporary society.
- We are to conclude that the writers of the Bible misunderstood what God intended.
- We are to claim the Bible is outdated and largely irrelevant.[34]
- We are to believe the Bible is out-of-date.[35]
- We must, therefore, examine the Bible's teachings and rethink our beliefs.

Are you a vocal counterculture to these things? Or are you one of those who just standby and say, "that's just the way it is?" Like the church in Laodicea, we have wall to wall people who are neither cold nor hot (see Rev. 3:14-22). The Laodiceans were not referred to as being *spiritually dead* nor as being *spiritually alive* .... They were indifferent:

- They were lost! For had they been "born again" they would not have been spued out of the mouth of Christ – who is the Head of the Church.

---

[34] Irrelevant means that something is not related to anything.

[35] Out-of-date means we have new ways of thinking and living today, so the Bible is out-of-date, your thinking and living up to this point is like reading a back-issue of newspaper.

- Had the church been totally cold, there would have been the possibility of reviving the coldness and the church might become hot again.

- The coldness and death of the church in Sardis, mixed with the weakness of the church in Philadelphia had produced the feeble, *lukewarm condition* of the Laodicean assembly. Total indifference to Christ marked the condition of the Laodiceans.

- The church in Laodicea was a group of undecided neutral members who would not take a stand one way or the other toward God, Christ, the Spirit, God's Word, nor His true people. This is a "Wake up call!"

- Total indifference today is probably damming more people to hell then drugs, alcohol, and all other sins combined. Today many like the Laodiceans, have no place for the Lord Jesus Christ or for those who are His. Are you rejected for your stand for Christ and truth?

Since each of the seven churches in Revelation represents a period in the history of the church between Pentecost and the Rapture – we recognize the fact that we are now living in a church age symbolized by *the spirit of the Laodiceans of John's Day.* The local church today is marked by the same indifference:

- Pride – God hates self-elevation.
- Wealth – state of the mind. America, things, money, looks, achievements, and pedigree.
- Consumerism – church shoppers.
- Self-satisfaction – only concerned about me (me-ism).
- Materialism – lots of stuff, think more of their stuff than God.
- Hedonism – seekers and lovers of pleasure and entertainment.

Though the Lord called men to shepherd his flock, sadly, every succeeding generation the people needed to look to the Lord as their shepherd and king. Additionally, the under shepherds needed to be watchful in following the Lord. Unfortunately, the weakness of human shepherds continued to be a major theme in Israel's history.

God as Shepherd

Today many church leaders insists that the use of the term shepherd to describe the concept of spiritual leadership is out-of-date or obsolete. Thus, the question arises, why don't we find a better way to communicate this spiritual model? First, there is no modern metaphor suitable for the task. Historically, whenever the church has chosen some picture other than the shepherd to describe spiritual leadership, error and decline has followed.

A humble shepherd serves as an adequate guide and safeguard to keep our leadership from abuses. Shepherds connect in a fundamental way to the very character and attributes of God. God is first called a shepherd in the opening book of the Bible. In Genesis 48:15 ESV, the shepherd Jacob called the Lord *"the God who has been my shepherd all my life to this day."* This initial reference to Jacob, the old deceiver, has reached the end of a life filled with discord and tenderness, poverty and riches, happiness, and deep sorrow. Earlier he had wrestled with the Lord. And received a new name, Israel, to mark his slow spiritual growth.

Jacob knew What it meant to be a shepherd! He spent twenty years on the job (see Genesis 31:40-41). He also knew that God had been with him every step of his troubled life. In fact, he was so confident in his divine Shepherd that he passed on the same confidence to his son Joseph (see Genesis 49:24).

No doubt the most famous of all the Old Testament descriptions of God as Shepherd is found in Psalm 23. In verse 1, David proclaims, *"The LORD is my shepherd, I shall not want."* Note the primary ways in which David compares God to a shepherd:

- He meets our needs (v. 1).
- He forces us to rest (v. 2).
- He brings us into life-giving surroundings (v. 2).
- He gives us peace (v. 2).
- He rejuvenates us when we're drained (v. 3).
- He enables us to live holy lives, to his everlasting praise (v. 3).
- He comforts us when death approaches (v. 4).
- He helps us to win over great opposition (v. 5).
- He blesses us in ways that leaves us breathless (v. 5).
- He fills us with confidence for this life and hope for the life to come (v. 6).

Jay Adams noted the following as he pondered this beloved psalm:

The name "pastoral" is a uniquely Christian term that expresses a fundamental concept that is deeply embedded in every biblical portrayal of Christian ministry. The term refers to a rich scriptural figure that finds its beginning and end in God. He who is the "Shepherd of Israel" (see Psalm 80:1), ultimately demonstrated the meaning of His covenantal love as the Great Shepherd of the sheep by giving His life for them (see John 10:11). The figure virtually bursts with significance, far more than didactic statements ever could express. Let us, therefore, try only to capture something of what it meant for David (a former shepherd) to write:

"The Lord is my Shepherd; I shall not want" (see Psalm 23:1), for in that declaration lies all that is meant by "Pastoral Work." To help to understand this, reread the sentence this way:

"The Lord is my Pastor; I shall not want" (Psalm 23:1).

The Shepherd is the one who provides full and complete care for all the sheep.[36]

Christ as Shepherd

In writing his gospel, Matthew apparently desired to not only emphasize Jesus' birthplace but also the shepherding aspects of His ministry. In Matthew 25:32 he depicts the Savior dividing His sheep like a shepherd, while in Matthew 26:31 he quotes Zechariah 13:7 to remind his readers that Jesus also suffered for the sake of His sheep. William Barclay accurately notes the greatest of all New Testament images is Jesus, the Good Shepherd.[37] This image of the shepherd is woven into the language and imagery of the Bible. This is seen especially in John 10 where Jesus makes the great claims for Himself in the Bible, such as:

- "I am the door of the sheep ... if anyone enters by me, he will be saved" (vv. 7,9 ESV).
- "I am the good shepherd" (v. 11 ESV).
- "I know my own sheep and my own sheep know me" (v. 14 ESV).
- "I lay down my life for the sheep" (v. 15 ESV).
- "I have other sheep that are not of this fold. I must bring them also" (v. 16 ESV).

---

[36] Jay E. Adams, *Shepherding God's Flock,* vol. 1, *The Pastoral Life* (Philadelphia: Presbyterian and Reformed, 1975) 5.

[37] William Barclay, *The Gospel of John,* vol. 2 (Daily Study Bible; Philadelphia: Westminster, 1975), 55.

- "They too will listen to my voice, and there shall be one flock and one shepherd" (v. 16 ESV).
- "You do not believe because you are not among my sheep" (v. 26 ESV).
- "My sheep hear my voice; and I know them, and they follow Me" (v. 27 ESV).
- "I give them eternal life, and they shall never perish" (v. 28 ESV).
- "No one can snatch them out of my hand" (v. 29 ESV).

The imagery takes on even greater importance once the reader gains an appreciation for the reality of shepherding in Judea. Judea was rough and stony country better for raising sheep than agricultural farming. John 10 has proven to be the favorite for millions of Christians throughout the ages. The image Jesus portrays there conveys all the warmth, security, strength, and hope for which every human heart desires.

Barclay tells the story of his friend who owned several sheep or perhaps it might be better to say his wife owned the sheep. One day they had to move. When the husband tried to load the sheep into the back of the truck – the sheep would not move. They dug in bleating and pulling away from him. They would not let him move them. But when the wife came out and spoke their names, immediately they followed her up into the back of the truck. Why? Because she was the one who cared for them, who healed them, who loved them. They knew her voice, and they trusted her voice. It was the voice of their shepherd.[38]

That is the exact picture Jesus painted of His intimate relationship with His sheep. Jesus knows his sheep, they know His voice, and they

---

[38] Ibid.

rest in His love for them, a love so extreme it led him to lay down His life for them. That is the Good Shepherd – and he is our preeminent model.

Jesus' self-image left such a deep impression on His disciples' consciousness that the New Testament Church could never get away from it. The writer of Hebrews begins to wind up the Book with a reference to *"our Lord Jesus, that great Shepherd of the sheep"* (Hebrews 13:20 ESV).

The apostle Peter, years after his conversation with His Lord, where Jesus charged him to *"Feed my lambs … Tend my sheep … Feed my sheep"* (see John 21:15, 16, 17 ESV), calls the Savior "the Shepherd and Overseer of your souls."

How fitting, then, that in the final book of the Bible, as in the first, the divine Shepherd makes His presence felt. In Revelation 7 an angel describes to the apostle John the blessed fate awaiting uncounted martyrs who stand before the throne of God:

> *He who sits on the throne will shelter them*
> *with his presence.*
> *They shall hunger no more,*
> *neither thirst anymore;*
> *the sun shall not strike them,*
> *nor any scorching heat.*
> *"For the Lamb in the midst of the throne will be their shepherd;*
> *He will guide them to springs of living water,*
> *and God will wipe away every tear from their eyes."*
> Revelation 7:15-17 (ESV)

Our only hope is faith in Jesus Christ. By His death, He satisfied the justice of God. He paid the penalty for sin in full. Praise God!

Moses as shepherd

It is not strange that many of the leaders God chose to lead and guide His people in the Old Testament spent a number of years training for their future roles by caring for flocks of sheep. The greatest of the Jewish leaders, Moses, learned invaluable lessons minding his father-in-law's sheep in the desert of Midian (see Exodus 3:1). God thought that the shepherd's life was the model life to prepare those men who would lead His people. God called Moses "the shepherd of His flock" through the prophet Isaiah" (see Isa. 63:11).

Moses was probably the hardest working man in Israel. He worked through three careers: **1)** privileged ruler in Egypt, **2)** forgotten shepherd in Midian, **3)** national liberator and shepherd leader of the Israelites. Throughout these pursuits Moses, constantly turned to God in prayer. Consider the following conversations he had with God:

- He debated with God concerning his fitness to lead Israel out of Egypt (see Exodus 3:11-4:17; 6:28-77).
- He interceded on behalf of the Egyptians (see Exodus 8:9-13).
- He asked for water for his thirsty nation of ex-slaves (see Exodus 15:24, 25).
- He pleaded with God about the sinful Hebrews and what God would do to them (see Exodus 32:11-13; 31-34).
- He interceded with God concerning his sister's leprosy, after she showed prejudice against his foreign-born wife (see Numbers 12:4-15).
- He prayed to God for the leadership transition of leadership to Joshua (see Numbers 27:15-27).
- He appealed to God to allow him to join his people in their entrance to the Promised Land (see Deuteronomy 3:23-25; 34:1-4).

Moses demonstrated the *often-forgotten truth* that God is more than ready to hear our complaints, appeals, and frustrations. Are you willing to approach God in prayer about the problems that upset you? Why not take a little break to do so right now?

Prayer is scary for many people. It is the kind of activity that they would preferably leave to the paid professionals. But Scripture encourages us with many examples of people who demonstrate prayer as an everyday activity for all of God's people. A case in point, Moses asked God for a successor:

> *"Let the LORD, the God of the spirits of all flesh, appoint a man over the congregation who shall go out before them and come in before them, who shall lead them out and bring them in, that the congregation of the LORD may not be as sheep that have no shepherd"* (Numbers 27:15-17 ESV).

The Lord granted Moses' request, and Joshua became not only the second leader of liberated Israel, but its second shepherd as well.

David as shepherd

If Moses was Israel's greatest leader, then David was its greatest king. He probably more than any other person in the Old Testament, earned the label "shepherd." Like Moses, he trained for his national leadership responsibilities as a shepherd. When the proper time arrived, the Lord told him, *"You shall be shepherd of my people Israel, and you shall be prince over Israel"* (2 Samuel 5:2 ESV).

David made a great impression on his people. He became known as a great leader – because he made a great shepherd. David was not remembered as much for his victorious military exploits or his political reforms as for his ability to shepherd his people with integrity of heart. A big part of what made David such an effective leader must have been the time he spent alone with his sheep – time he could use to meditate on his relationship with God. In his youth, David had plenty of time alone, time to meet with God and get to know Him.

At times the sheep would grow still and quiet – that's when a wise shepherd gets to know his God [the time for reflection, study, and prayer]. While Jesus was never a shepherd by vocation, he continually practiced this discipline of getting away to commune with God.

After caring for his sheep in the field all day, David knew their needs. He did not have to wonder how he could minister to the flock. In his meditation, David thought about God, but in a way that was *rooted* in his daily life. Good theology doesn't drift from here to there. It is *rooted* in the problems, difficulties, and circumstances of real life. O, how many pastors are missing that point. Have you ever wondered, how much of David's theological reflection in the Psalms comes out of his shepherding experiences, lifestyle, and worldview? It's obvious that his son, Solomon's writings do not have the depth we see in David.

When David got off track with Bathsheba, he wandered away after committing adultery with her, and he refused to repent for more than a year. How did God get his attention? By pricking his shepherd's heart. The prophet Nathan told David a story about a wealthy man who had killed a poor family's one sheep so that he would not have to sacrifice one of his own. David went berserk! "The man doesn't deserve to live!" He shouted. A little later, Nathan replied, "You are the man!" At last, a chance to repent and to restore his relationship with God; and that happened when Nathan brought the king back to his shepherd's roots (see 2 Samuel 12:1-13).

Nathan broke David's heart by appealing to his shepherd's heart.

STUDY GUIDE: CHAPTER 13 WHO ARE WE BECOMING?

1. The pandemic has caused the church to reexamine the _____ _____ serves the _____ of believers.

2. True righteousness is of God, any other _____ is _____.

3. There are two approaches to receiving the righteousness of God. One common approach is to try to earn righteousness or right standing with God is through _____.

4. The second and only true approach to righteousness that works is that we must receive it as a gift of _____.

5. Explain the indifference in the churches of Sardis and Laodicea as compared with the sins facing the church today.

6. Good theology is rooted in the problems, difficulties, and circumstances of _____ _____.

7. Much of David's theological reflection in the Psalms came out of his _____ _____, lifestyle, and worldview.

SECTION THREE
THE GLORY OF THE SHEPHERD

"I will give shepherds after my own heart, who will lead you with knowledge and understanding" (Jeremiah 3:15).

CHAPTER FOURTEEN

> *"So, I exhort the elders among you, as a fellow elder and a witness of the sufferings of Christ, as well as a partaker in the glory that is going to be revealed; shepherd the flock of God that is among you, exercising oversight, not under compulsion, but willingly, as God would have you; not for shameful gain, but eagerly; not domineering over those in your charge, but being examples to the flock"* (1 Peter 5:1-3 ESV).

Many in the Western world reject the shepherd's model of ministering because they consider it to be primitive, outdated, and unsophisticated. However, I hope you have begun to see that the traits of the shepherd as laid out in the biblical model are exactly what people are seeking today. They want:

> relationships
> connectedness
> security

feel as if they matter

want to feel loved

Does the shepherd model mean that the pastor must go back to being the primary visitor to the congregation? Emphatically no! Ephesian 4 instructs us to equip the sheep for the work of the ministry, and that includes visiting.

Just because something has been practiced for five hundred years does mean it is right – Likewise, just because something has not been practiced for five hundred years does not mean it is wrong!

Jesus viewed himself as a shepherd and saw his people as sheep, yet he spent much of his time with three of the twelve. As pastor, I have the primary responsibility to train, equip, (preaching and teaching) and shepherd certain members. I also need to walk among the rest of the sheep. I can't always be with the deacons and other leaders. As shepherd, I must be proactive in getting in touch with a broader base of my sheep.

Through my years of pastoring, I have noticed how strange some people have looked at my wife, as she would get together with people who are not from amongst the so called "church family" of the congregation. Here's their approach, "We saw your wife with that "odd family." That means, "the family is not of the social status we prefer for our first lady associating with."

The other flock

There are "other sheep" we *need* to know besides the leadership. The other sheep are the Gentiles, who were not in the Jewish fold.

Jesus must bring them, and He will do it through His voice. His Word. We see this happening in Acts 10 when Peter went to the Gentiles and preached the Word; they believed and were saved. Verse 16 can be read, "and there shall be one flock [the church] and one Shepherd [Christ]." The body of Christ is made up of Jews and Gentiles who trust Christ, and there is one body, one flock, one common spiritual life (see Eph. 2:11-22; 3:1-13; 4:1-16).

I need to hear what is actually going on among all of the flock as we ensure that all are properly shepherded. Although the Bible distinguishes between the sheep and the shepherd, it maintains a picture of the shepherd constantly walking among the flock. The shepherd is able to touch the individual sheep and know that they are his. The flock can *hear* the shepherd's voice; they know it is their shepherd and they *follow* their shepherd by faith.

Called to be shepherds

I personally believe God is still calling the leaders of *his* people to become shepherds. Listen again to his ancient but *ever-new* commands:

- "Shepherd your people with your staff, the flock of your inheritance" (Micah 7:14 ESV).
- "Pay careful attention to yourselves and to your flock in which the Holy Spirit has made you overseers, to care for the church of God, which he obtained with his own blood" (Acts 20:28 ESV).
- "Shepherd the flock of God that is among you, exercising oversight, not under compulsion, but willingly, as God would have you; not for shameful gain, but eagerly" (1 Peter 5:2 ESV).

Don't be mere leaders, strive to be shepherds. We are to be shepherds of the church of God – which He bought with His own blood. Even today God says, "I shed my blood for them." They are My sheep. Therefore, you shepherd them, care for them, and love them – just as He modeled before you!

Where have all the shepherds gone?

I read about one very influential church leader remarking after a meeting on "the decline of the American church," boldly declaring that our problem is that "We have too many pastors (shepherds) and not enough leaders." Whatever, his thoughts about pastors are, they are the problem; and to him the solution to the problem is more leaders. Certainly, that is the popular conclusion today. And though we have no lack of books, curricula, and other resources – still much of the African American church remains on life support. Why?

I'm sure we will agree the "leader model" *is* the *current* favorite – and this is the reason all the shepherds are gone. Without a standard the leader model has appeared in the church in various (individual) forms and styles as do leaders themselves. Therefore, the end results are many books, practices, and perceptions on church leadership. Most pastors in the Black Church will not associate with the sheep, because of some distorted view actually borrowed from the leader model.

We minister out of our identity

I am convinced that many of us struggle with ministry because we have no clear idea of who we are as pastors. We all operate out of a sense of identity, but if we are not clear about that identity, we find ourselves in a mess (where much of the Church is today). I also believe that when people (especially pastors) attempt to minister outside of their identities, absolutely no amount of tricks or gimmicks can take up the slack.

Without a firm identity of who we are and what we are called to do, we'll just waste time blindly running in place (treadmill) following every fad that comes our way – and we continue "in our own strength" frustrated and ineffective. Clearly, the answer to this malady *will not be* strictly human and come in the form of therapy or some sense of higher self-esteem. That is not the answer to people who are created by God and born again by the Spirit from above. Our identity must be filled with Christian content – that is rooted in God, formed by Christ, and empowered by the Holy Spirit. Certainly, for Christian pastors, the question of our identity, our sense of calling, our mission in life must be grounded in Scripture and filled with theological integrity.

So, who we are determines what we are to *do*. Let's consider how the implications that different identities present for our ministry priorities:

- If God has called us to be *leaders,* then our priority becomes goals, objectives, and the bottom line.
- If God has called us to be *managers,* then our priority becomes structure, systems, order, and keeping everything under control.
- If God has called us to be *CEO's,* then our priority becomes developing a vision and issuing orders.
- If God has called us to be *shepherds,* then our priority becomes caring for, feeding, and correcting the sheep.

Certainly, you can't do it all. Therefore, the first question we must answer is what has God called us to be? Everything else will flow from our answer to that question.

There are various words and images in the Scripture to describe the people whom God uses. He calls us:

- Servants (Matthew 24:45)
- Workers (Matthew 9:37)

- Stewards (1 Corinthians 4:1, KJV)
- Managers (Luke 12:42)
- Priests (Revelation 1:6)
- Kings (I Corinthians 4:8)
- Royalty (I Peter 2:9).

Who does God say we are?

When all is said and done, it is obvious that the (most popular), the leader model *is not* adequate. While much good has resulted from the many conferences, workshops, and books written on leadership in the church, many of them miss the mark of the high calling of God. Though, my statement would probably be questionable to some, and maybe so – that is, if the current best-sellers lists were really adequate indicators. Certainly, they are not adequate. Adding to all of that has been discussed, we must consider the functions formulated by human brains and hands.

I pray that by now your spirit resonates with the biblical model of pastor as shepherd. Once again, God has given us a splendid model of what it means to be a shepherd of the sheep (Jesus Christ). What we need in this epidemic prone season are God-empowered churches led by Spirit-filled, and caring shepherds, because God loves His shepherds. Does God ever say, "Pastors, here is your governing model?" I believe He does! The apostle Peter lays it out for us in (I Peter 5:1-4), the one image that rises above all others to help is define our *biblical model (role)*:

To the elders among you, I appeal as a fellow elder, a witness of Christ's sufferings and one who also will share in the glory to be revealed: **Be shepherds of God's flock** *that is under your care, serving as overseers – not because you must, but because you are willing, as God wants you to be; not greedy for money, but eager to serve; not lording it over those who entrusted to you, but* *being examples to the flock. And when the Chief Shepherd appears, you will receive the crown of glory that will never fade away.*

Peter entreats his pastoral readers to be *shepherds of God's flock*. He didn't urge them to be priests, or kings or leaders, or managers, or even servants. He strongly appealed to them to be shepherds. Peter isn't the only New Testament writer to see the importance of pastor as shepherd. Listen to the apostle Paul addressing the elders of the church at Ephesus:

> *"Pay careful attention yourselves and to all the flock in which the Holy Spirit has made you overseers, to care for the church of God, which he obtained with his own blood. I know that after my departure fierce wolves will come in among you, not sparing the flock"* (Acts 20;28-29 ESV).

As before, these leaders are called "elders" and "overseers," but they are commanded to behave as "shepherds." Paul seems to think of "elder" and "overseer" as job titles, but he urges these men to adopt "shepherd" as their central model of ministry. It important that we distinguish between form and function, though we often confuse the two. I don't believe God uses terms loosely. There must be something within the image of a shepherd that ought to capture and hold our hearts.

As the pendulum swings

Throughout church history the pendulum of Christ-centeredness and adherence to the New Covenant has moved to the left of center or to the right of center. These positions represent major changes in the church throughout the generations. As I stated earlier, change happens over several generations or more. Because a thing has not been used for 2000 years does not mean it is wrong, and although a thing has been used for 2000 years does not mean it is right. Though we find shepherds today in different parts of the world and some in America, most people think they are outdated. Christ identified Himself, the Chief Shepherd. I have never read in the Bible that He at some point would no longer be necessary.

STUDY GUIDE: CHAPTER 14 WHERE HAVE ALL THE SHEPHERDS GONE?

1. Although the shepherd's model is considered outdated and unsophisticated, however, the 5 traits of the shepherd are laid out in this biblical model. List: _____ _____ _____ _____ _____.

2. The body of Christ is made up of _____, and _____, and there is one body, one flock, one common spiritual life.

3. I'm sure we all will agree that the "leader model" is the _____ _____ and this is the reason all the shepherds are gone.

4. When all is said and done, the leader model is _____ _____.

5. Peter is not the only one who see the pastor as the _____ _____.

6. Called elders and overseers, but they are to believe as _____.

7. Since Christ identified Himself as Chief Shepherd, is there any doubt?

CHAPTER FIFTEEN
THE GOOD SHEPHERD

"I am the good shepherd; I know my sheep and my sheep know me. Just as the Father knows me and I know the Father − and I lay down my life for the sheep. I have other sheep that are not of this sheep that are not of this sheep pin. I must bring them also. They too will listen to my voice, and there shall be one flock and one shepherd" (John 10:14-16 NIV).

In the gospel of John, Jesus declares, "I am the Good Shepherd" (John 10:11, 14 NIV). These words were familiar to his original audiences. Not only were his listeners familiar with the vocation of the shepherd, but they heard Jesus' identification with the Lord, Israel's Shepherd. He then, declares himself to be the Shepherd-King who had been prophesied by *Ezekiel and Jeremiah*. Where human shepherds had failed, Jesus, God incarnate, would succeed.

Jesus uses shepherding *imagery* to describe his relationship with the sheep. *"I am the good shepherd; and I know my sheep and am known by*

My own" (John 10:14 NIV). Who are his sheep? Jesus makes this point clear, that the identifying mark of his sheep is that they hear his voice. *"Hearing"* is more than mere auditory sounds, but a deep, spiritual understanding that responds to faith. *"My sheep listen to my voice; I know them, and they follow me. I give them eternal life, and they shall never perish; no one can snatch them out of my hand"* (John 10:27-29 NIV). The effectual call of the Good Shepherd draws his sheep into the safety of his sheepfold. The ultimate identification of the sheep as sheep is determined in the sovereign plan of God.

Jesus as the shepherd provides not some but all the care his sheep need. He knows that their needs go much deeper than just feeding them bread, which only faith in him could supply. Jesus said to them, "I am the bread of life; whoever comes to me shall not hunger, and whoever believes in me shall never thirst" (John 6:35 ESV). His sheep will find *all* of their sustenance in him and his Word as they follow on and walk with Him.

Jesus not only provides for his sheep, but he *calls* them to follow him wherever he leads them. A mark of true discipleship is that they follow their shepherd. That truth is sounded in the call of the very first apostles. He said, to them, "Follow Me, and I will make you *"fishers of men"* (Matthew 4:19 ESV). Emphasis added throughout.

Jesus also emphasized that, "If anyone would come after Me, let him deny himself and take up his cross daily and follow Me" (Luke 9:23 ESV). Jesus goes on ahead to prepare a place for his sheep with that where he is there they may follow (see John 14:2-6). Earlier in John's gospel, Jesus uses familiar shepherding imagery as he describes himself as "the door to the sheep" (see John 10:7).

Here He signifies the exclusive means of entrance into the flock. "I am the door; if anyone enters by Me, he will be saved and will go in and out and will find pasture"(John 10:9 ESV). Only those who enter through Him will enjoy the full care that only He can provide.

Christ is the Good Shepherd

Christ is the Good Shepherd who *died* for His sheep! In the Old Testament the sheep *died* for the shepherd! In the New Testament the Shepherd died for the sheep. He calls through His Word, and those who believe step through the Door, out of their religious fold, into the true flock of Christ – the body of Christ. Two or three months later the Jews were still arguing with Jesus about His comment! He pointed out to them that they were not "of His sheep" and therefore could not believe. Here He gives a description of true Christians – His sheep:

1. *They hear His voice, which means they hear His Word and positively respond to it.* Unsaved people have little or no interest in the Bible – true sheep live in the Word.

2. *They know Christ and are known (John 10:14, 27), so that they will not follow a false shepherd.* Church members who run from one religious system to another or one cult to another are proving they are not true sheep.

3. *They follow Christ, which speaks of obedience.* No one has a right to claim to be one of Christ's sheep if he or she lives in willful, persistent, open disobedience, and refuses to do something about it. Just as there are false shepherds, so there are goats who try to pass for sheep. One day Christ will say to them, "I never knew you" (Matt. 7:23 ESV).

4. *They have eternal life and are secure.* The Scripture declares the wonderful security true believers have in Christ. We have eternal life, not just life. We are in Christ's care and the Father's hand, a double assurance for His sheep. We are the Father's gift to His Son, and the Father will not take back a gift.

Sheep are a beautiful illustration of Christians.

- Sheep are clean animals and Christians have been cleansed from sin.
- Sheep flock together, and so do true Christians.
- Sheep are harmless, and Christians should be blameless and harmless.
- Sheep are given to wander, and so are we.
- Sheep need a shepherd for protection, guidance, and food, Christians need Christ for spiritual protection, daily guidance, and spiritual food.
- Sheep are useful and productive; so are true Christians.
- Sheep were used for sacrifices; and Christians are willing to yield themselves for Christ as "living sacrifices" (see Romans 12:1).

The Jews proved their unbelief by trying to kill Christ. He refuted their claims by quoting (see Psalm 82:6). If Christ called earthly judges "god," then surely, He could call Himself the Son of God! Christ then left the scene; and many came to Him and put their faith in Him. By faith, they stepped through the Door, out of the Jewish religious fold, and into the freedom and eternal life Christ alone can give.

STUDY GUIDE: CHAPTER 15 THE GOOD SHEPHERD

1. Jesus declared to be the _____ _____ who had been prophesied by _____ and _____.

2. Jesus uses shepherding imagery to describe His relationship with the sheep. Who are My sheep? Jesus makes this point clear, that the identifying mark of His sheep is that they _____ _____ _____.

3. Christ is the Good Shepherd who died for His sheep. In the Old Testament the sheep died for the shepherd. In the New Testament the Shepherd died for the sheep.

4. True Christians hear His voice meaning they hear His _____. They know Christ and are known of Him, so they will not follow a _____ _____. They follow Christ – which speaks of _____. They have eternal life and are _____.

5. Only those who enter through Christ will enjoy the _____ _____ that only He can provide.

6. We are the Father's gift to _____ _____ and the Father will not _____ _____ _____ _____.

7. Sheep were used for sacrifices; and Christians are willing to yield themselves for _____ as _____ _____.

CHAPTER SIXTEEN
THE OPPORTUNITY TO SHINE

And He gave the apostles, the prophets, the evangelists, the shepherds, and teachers, to equip the saints for the work of ministry, for building up of the body of Christ, until we all attain to the unity of the faith, and of the knowledge of the Son of God, to matured manhood, to the measure of the stature of the fulness of Christ. So that, we may no longer be children, tossed to and fro by the waves, and carried about by every wind of doctrine, by human cunning, by craftiness in deceitful schemes. Rather, speaking the truth in love, we are to grow up in every way into Him, who is the head, into Christ, from whom the whole body, joined and held together by every joint with which of each it is equipped, when each part is working properly, makes the body grow so that it builds itself up in love (Ephesians 4:11-16 ESV).

In the Scripture above, Paul laid out the operation orders for the under shepherd (pastors). Scripture continually alerts its readers to watch for spiritual counterfeits.[39] We can readily see the importance of discernment today as we look back at the Old Testament prophets who warned Israel about false prophets, even rebuking the nation when they strayed following a false leader rather than a true leader. While not as dramatic as the Old Testament prophet; the New Testament also warns against deceptive and misleading false leaders.

Leaders versus shepherds

I believe that God is raising up a generation of New Testament leading and teaching shepherds (see Ephesians 4:11), in this very hour to rebuke and warn our churches and America! Are we Listening? Likewise, I believe God is raising up a new breed of (disciples) *believers* [a new wineskin], who will prophesy, pray, preach, teach, bind, and loose.[40] These believers know that when the enemy comes in like a flood, the Spirit of the Lord will raise up a standard against him (see Isaiah 59:19).

Every succeeding generation in history has proven the need for this warning! The true shepherd must warn and protect the flock from such deceit. In spite of God's loving care and safe guiding – soon changes begin to take place. This happens when a leader model is selected rather than a biblical shepherd model for a leader. Although the terms leader and shepherd partially overlap in meaning these two leaders' approaches are not identical. The essential differences between these two ministry models is the fact that the leader model will never transform the culture around it.

Only a shepherd model can attain that. That is why God calls us to be shepherds and not leaders – leaders are man-made, while shepherds

---

[39] The New Testament has exposed the "false" on many occasions such as: (1) false apostles (2 Cor. 11:13), (2) false brethren (2 Cor. 11:26; Gal. 2:4, (3) false Christs (Matt. 24:24), (4) false prophets (Matt. 24:11; 2 Pet. 2;1; I John 4:1), (5) false teachers (2 Pet. 2:1), and (6) false witnesses (Matt. 26:60; Acts 6:13).

[40] These believers know that no weapon formed against them will prosper.

are God-called. To the leader model people are a means to an end. To the shepherd people are a priority. A leader turns people into numbers to meet a certain end (the mission is more important than the people; love and care for the people is not their problem). While a shepherd loves and knows the flock and the flock knows the shepherd (1st priority) personally, without the people there can be no successful mission.

Like old Israel, over a period of time much of the church has moved from the center of God's will to the outer fringes. The Holy Spirit and His ministries are replaced with idolatry, external rituals, and ceremonies. Throughout Church history various interventions are recorded which God has instituted or used in the world to call His church back to the center (follow Christ in the New Covenant).[41]

The true church must be visible

Especially during these trying times, the church should be shining – and coming to the rescue of people, because we have Jesus! Our Lord said we Christians "are the light of the world," set on a hill – not hiding at home nor behind the closed doors of the church. In Revelation 2, Jesus commended the church in Ephesus for their faith and perseverance under hard circumstances. Then, He continued with a warning to them and to us today:

> *"But I have this against you, that you have abandoned the love you had at first. Remember therefore from where you have fallen and repent and do the works you did at first; if not, I will come to you and remove your lampstand from its place, unless you repent"* (Revelation 2:4-5 ESV).

A lampstand means influence and place in society. If we look back, we know that the lampstand at Ephesus was removed. Are we doing

---

[41] Jay Leach, *The Apostolic Rising* (Trafford Publishing, 2021) 75

kingdom work? Again, the true church has got to be visible. When it comes to God's truth – there is no neutral position. I really believe people are searching for something that transcends their difficulties and present circumstances of their lives. Jesus is the only hope for the sinner to be saved and receive eternal life.

Daily we are seeing every aspect of our culture moving further and further away from biblical principles – but God's Word has not changed. As Satan stirs up more hatred, censoring, and increases social and political pressure against believers, the Lord will probably use them as a means to discipline and refine the true church. We need to stand in bold allegiance to our Lord and Savior, Jesus Christ.

America is making up her own rules – and her own laws.

The world may not appreciate the preciousness of Christianity, and a part of the blame for that belongs to us believers. As the final hour draws near, it's time to recognize the evil agendas, plans, the (one world) globalists are plotting for in their next move. It not only includes their ongoing operation to rid the world of Christians and Christianity, but also to destroy the institutions of this country such as government, education, marriage and the family and remake them all in their image.

The spirit of antichrist under Satan's command and guidance is on the move carrying out his evil intentions which are becoming clearer each day. We must not be ignorant of the enemy's schemes or surprised at the rapid increase of criminal activities, disrespect of authority, conspiracy theories, evil, and lawlessness across this nation and throughout the world. As I am writing this book, variants of the COVID-19 continue to bring more fear and more confusion. All of the policies and restrictions put in place have affected our freedoms, the economy, our relationships, the elderly, our children, movement and travel, our church gatherings and so much more of daily life has been placed into the hands of science, reason, and the media.

Earlier, I stated that research has shown that 70% of America's top scientists in America are atheists. Is our lampstand being removed from the American church? The culture in this country is going downhill fast; with the loss of respect for authority, and the basis upon which authoritative moral standards can be asserted in the public square or in the church has disappeared also. If there are no moral law and standards – there is nothing to enforce. Why? Because there is nothing wrong. Is it possible that this idea has gotten into the church?

If the boundaries have vanished between truth and falsehood in doctrine, then the boundaries of right and wrong have given way to a "moral emptiness" also. This being true, then there would be those who would stand against those who oppose immorality. We live in a day of diversity and tolerance, where God has been dethroned, and to denounce "sin" will soon be challenged. To stand in opposition to *anything* that others hold dear makes you a bigot and a hate monger. Accordingly, this implies that church leaders that advocate certain aberrant lifestyles are in no position to *discipline* members who engage such lifestyles.

"The germ of dissolution of our federal government is in ... the federal judiciary, an irresponsible body ... working like gravity by night and by day, gaining a little today and a little tomorrow, and advancing its noiseless step like a thief, over the field of jurisdiction ..."[42] – Thomas Jefferson in 1821

If the standards are up to the "self" there is no ground upon which the church can stand to exercise discipline. Why would one who

---

[42] William J. Federer, *Backfired* (Ameri search, Inc., St. Louis, MO, 2010) 231

has preempted God from their memory be interested in church? (see Romans 1:19-21). The Bible is 100% the standard, and we stand on it, because it is truth.

How can we agree with anything else? I believe as shepherds of the flock of God, we may have to face litigation for exercising our biblical responsibilities of church disciplines. Social media has censored me three times for what they claimed was "being too political" and "offensive."

Corrupt judges

Today, judges have redefined the word "church" to mean *"anything and all religious activity or acknowledgment."*[43] We can look forward to suffering immensely for standing not in your truth or my truth, but in the truth of God's Word! Let the redeemed of the Lord, "say so!"

Watching the daily news — is it not strange the love, trust, and respect America is giving to secular science and reason (scientists) these days, especially when neither will give God a favorable mention? Are we raising up the man of sin?[44] Down through the centuries, kings, presidents, and other potentates have been thought to be this "man of sin (lawlessness)," especially when the individual is unpopular with the people.

---

[43] Ibid. 230

[44] The order of end time events: **(1)** The mystery of lawlessness under divine restraint which had already begun in the apostles' time (v.7). **(2)** The apostasy of the professing church (v.3; Lk. 18:8; 2 Timothy 3:1-8); **(3)** The removal of that which restrains the mystery of lawlessness (vs. 6,7). The restrainer is a person – "he," none other than the Holy Spirit in the church to be "taken out of the way" (v.7; 1 Thess. 4:14-17); **(4)** The manifestation of the lawless one (vs. 8-10; Dan. 7:8; 9:12; Mt. 24:15; Rev. 13:2-10; **(5)** The coming of Christ in glory and the destruction of the lawless one (v.8; Rev. 19:11-21); **(6)** The Day of the Lord (vs. 9-12; Isa. 2:12 KJV Ref.).

The falling away

> "Let no one deceive you by any means; for that Day will not
> come unless the falling away comes first, and the man of sin is
> revealed, the son of perdition. Who opposes and exalts himself
> above all that is called God or that is worshipped, so that he
> sits as God in the temple of God, showing himself that he is
> God. Do you not remember that when I was still with you, I
> told you these things."[45]

The word "apostasy" means "a falling away." Here it refers to
a falling away from the truth of the Word of God. Certainly, there
were false teachers in Paul's day, but the apostolic church was united
on the truths of the Word of God. Wherever you ran into a Christian
he or she believed in the Word of God, the deity of Christ, and the
"Christian unbelief;" people say they are Christians, yet deny deity
of Christ, the inspiration of the Bible, and the things of God. This
apostasy or falling away from the truth is promised in 1 Timothy 4 and
2 Timothy 3. We are living in *apostate days right now*, which announces
that the coming of the Lord is near. The Professing but not possessing
church has departed from the faith.

Paul promises the rise of a world dictator, "man of sin" …. The
son of perdition (v. 3). He is not speaking of a world system, but a
person who will lead a world system, the "man of sin." This "man of
sin" contrasts with Christ, the Savior from sin:

- He is the son of perdition – Christ is the Son of God.
- He is the liar – Christ is the Truth.

This world ruler will be energized by the devil and will unite
nations in a great federation (the ten horns of Daniel's image, Daniel

---

[45] 2 Thessalonians 2:3-5.

7). According to Revelation 17, the Antichrist will cooperate with the apostate world church in his rise to power, and then he will destroy this religious system when he no longer need them. The program follows:

1. The true church will be raptured.

2. The Antichrist will begin to rise to power in a peaceful manner.

3. He will unite Europe and make a seven-year covenant with Israel to protect it (see Daniel 9). Back in the early 1970's when I was in Bible College, I loved the study of prophecy. America could not be found as a player in the Tribulation.

4. In all probability America and Europe will be the spearhead of the Antichrist army, if not reduced to total insignificance beforehand. We are going down the tube as a nation at a rapid speed. Still, our hope remains in Jesus Christ.

5. After three and one-half years Antichrist will break the covenant and invade Israel. I believe the United States and Europe will probably provide the spearhead units.

6. At the end of the seven-year tribulation period (Day of the Lord), Christ will return to earth and destroy the Antichrist and his system.

Both the Old Testament and the New Testament predict the return of the Jews to Palestine and the rebuilding of the temple. It has been reported that all the materials are hand to build the temple. It has been reported that they already have a red heifer on hand. The Antichrist will set himself up in the temple, which marks the "abomination of desolation" (see Daniel 11:31; Matthew 24:15).

The completion of the Church

The Day of the Lord applies to the Gentiles and the Jews, but not the church. It is a day of wrath, and the church is not destined for wrath (see 1 Thessalonians 1:10; 5:9). The purpose of the Tribulation is the judgment of the Gentile nations and the purification of Israel – which by this time is back in their own land, still in unbelief. Antichrist cannot begin his rise to power until after the church is raptured from the earth. Notice the contrast between the church and Antichrist's followers:

- We have been saved by believing the Truth; Satan's followers are damned because they believe the lie.
- We have believed the good news of the Gospel; they believe the false promises of the devil.
- We are destined for the glory of heaven; they are destined for hell.

Paul urged the church then and us today, in all of this to: "Stand fast!" Don't be moved by all of the world convulsions, political upheavals, conspiracy theories, and religious apostasy. All of those things *must* take place before the end as prophesied in the Old and new Testaments – but be reminded God is still on the throne. Be aware, as the end of the age approaches, it will be more difficult to live for Christ and serve Him. What are Christians to do?

- Hold on to the Word of God (in your heart).
- Our hope is in Christ and His Word.
- Keep on giving out the Word.
- Keep on working for Christ.
- Maintain prayer discipline.

As we win others to Christ and make disciples, we are building up the body of Christ. Upon completion of the body, it will be "caught up to glory." This is what Peter had in mind by "hastening the coming of the day of God" (2 Peter 3:11-12). As long as the church is in the world, Satan's evil plans and programs of wickedness are put on hold.

I believe Satan has to prepare an antichrist in every generation, because he knows not the day nor the hour – but he knows his time is short! Once the church is gone, Satan will have more freedom to try and destroy Israel and contaminate humankind. The two-part second coming of Christ is more than a doctrine to look at and study. It is "Truth" to grip our lives and make us better Christians.

> It is not enough to know about His coming or to believe it; we must practice it daily.

Pray and be patient

Though Satan is at work in the world, we can still pray to God and see Him answer. The only way to counteract Satan's lies is to share the truth of the Word of God. The Word of God is living (see Hebrews 4:12). As shepherds, we move forward with the Gospel, we know that Satan will raise up perverse and evil people to oppose us (see Acts 18:1-12).

We must be patient as we pray and give out the Gospel of Christ. Remember, we cannot trust humankind, but we can trust our faithful Lord and Savior, Jesus Christ. Let's be found faithful when Christ comes, and we stand before Him. As prayer leaders today often seek God for the "transformation of cities," urging faith to seek God for a whole city, how are we to be guided in our intercession?" In 1 John 5:14, 15, we read *that if we ask anything according to God's will,* **we can have confidence He will answer us.**

In 2 Thessalonians 3:1, God's Word reveals His desire for His work to *advance everywhere* in the way it had advanced in Thessalonica. We have the authority of the Scriptures to pray boldly for the gospel to "run *swiftly* and be glorified," just as it was in *that city* the Holy Spirit impacted long ago – the very city where the charge was made that the gospel had "turned their world upside down" (see Acts 17:6).

Certainly, it can be no accident that the Scriptures encourages prayer for "city transformation." It is biblical to believe for a move of the gospel that will not only change you, your family, your church, and your city, but one that will cause that grace to *spread a testimony* far beyond your home (see 1 Thess. 1:6, 7; Eph. 3:14-21). While we have the opportunity the church must put forth every effort including social media to get the true gospel out!

STUDY GUIDE: CHAPTER 16 THE OPPORTUNITY TO SHINE

1. Scripture continuously alerts its readers to watch for
   _____ _____.

2. And Although the terms leader model and biblical shepherd model
   partially overlap in meaning these two leader approaches are not
   identical. The essential differences between the two ministry
   models is that the leader model will never _____ the
   _____ around it.

3. Throughout church history various interventions are recorded
   which God has instituted or used in the world to _____ His
   church back to the _____.

4. Today judges have redefined the word "church" to mean
   "anything and all religious activity or acknowledgment."

5. The word apostasy means "a falling away." Here it refers to a
   falling away from the truth of God's Word.

6. It is not enough to know about His coming or to believe it; we
   must _____ it daily.

7. In Thessalonians 3:1, God's Word reveals His desire
   for His work to advance everywhere in the way it had
   advanced in _____.

CHAPTER SEVENTEEN
THE GOSPEL FLOW

"Therefore remember that you, once Gentiles in the flesh – who are called Uncircumcision by what is called "the Circumcision made in the flesh by hands – that at that time you were without Christ, being aliens from the commonwealth of Israel and strangers from the covenants of promise having no hope and without God in the world. But now in Christ Jesus you who once were far off have been brought near by the blood of Christ. For He Himself is our peace, who has made one, and has broken down the middle wall of separation, having abolished in His flesh the enmity, that is the law of commandments contained in ordinances, so as to create in Himself one new man from the two, thus making peace, and that He might "reconcile them both to God in one body through the cross, thereby putting to death the enmity. And He came and preached peace to you who were afar off and to those who were near. For through Him we both have access by one

Spirit to the Father. So then you are no longer strangers and aliens, but you are fellow citizens with the saints and members of the household of God (Ephesians 2:11-22 NKJV).

Back in the early 70's, I went through the "Jungle Survival Course" at the Jungle Operation Training Center in the Republic of Panama. It was much different warfare then I experienced in the years 1967 and 68 in Vietnam operating in a unit of the 25th Infantry Division. Although we were in combat our supply lines were never cut off. Air Force C-130 aircrafts, Army helicopters, and trucks supplied our needs including clean potable water. In the jungle of Panama there were no planes or helicopters to come to our rescue. We were broken down into three man-teams and sent out on separate mission in the jungle for several days, we had to survive off the land for food and water.

We departed as a 3-man team, and we had to return as a 3-man team. In prep training before taking off we spent time making ropes, fashioning spears, learning to identify edible plants and animals. But the main topic was *water without which we could not survive*! Now consider just how crucial it is to be cleansed by the *water* of the Word of the God in sanctification and living a mature Christian life. Like drinking water turned out to be the most important concern – the truth of God's Word keeps us alive and growing [when we plant (sow) it in our hearts], prayerfully watch over it, meditate on it day and night, and obediently keep it in practice.

Our bodies can survive a week without food, but they can't go more than several days (some people less) without clean water in the jungle. So one of the primary concerns to surviving the jungle is learning to find and collect clean water. Water can be found in some of the most unusual places. But you learn also that all water is not healthy to drink. It's very important to remember that stagnant or dead water kills people!

When looking for water, it is vital to always search for places where the water is not stagnant. We learned that stagnant water has significantly lower oxygen, which absorbs dangerous bacteria and larvae. You recognize stagnant or dead water by the terrible stench or aroma it puts off. Flowing water, however, has a continual source of oxygen, which keeps the water more free from harmful elements, making it a safe place from which to get it. The key to a successful mission in the jungle operation was three of us started out (meshed together as one) and we had to complete the course together (meshed together as one) – no man left behind!

While methods change – truth *always* remains the same.

Have you ever sat in a church and wondered, "Why does this feel so dead?" The early church of the New Testament knew nothing of such a feeling, because they were on a life mission, "Go!" Don't just sit there. "Go make disciples!" Keep moving forward in faith! Obey God's Spirit and Word (action)! In conversing with our pastors and churches on how to build biblical community, I am amazed by the separated gospel many pastors have built into the minds and hearts of their people.

The structure of their ministry really shows when there is higher priority given to a church's *non-essential* (activities) program; than given to *essential* deeper spiritual relationships "in Christ." When more time is spent branding the church's programed program than training lay leaders, they are shocked at the shallowness in the church's spiritual outcomes. This condition is typical of any church where the Holy Spirit and the Word are denied priority.

The people may exude a righteous desire to immerse themselves in the deeper waters of biblical community, but all we have to give them is a shallow dead creek formed by the last rainstorm. How can our people go deeper in such shallow water? As shepherd pastors we have the responsibility to lead our people toward "spiritual transformation in Christ," while preparing them for heaven. Sadly, this shallowness has overshadowed much of the Church in America. Our ability to *change* this is limited only by our *understanding of the Gospel*!

Many secular-minded people find it easier to believe their own perceptions of the circumstances or what "people in the street" has to say about the situation, than to (obediently) search the Scriptures for the truth of God's Word. Like the water source in the jungle, a shallow church where the gospel is stagnant will always have a stench of death – such a church is not a source for spiritual life! In the spiritual family what binds us together is no longer socioeconomic status, race, ethnicity, or location. The gospel is what links the members of the spiritual family together. We have been set free by the blood of the cross – you and I no longer live, but Christ lives within and through us. Have you heard it said lately, "the true gospel of Christ will either draw you or drive you?" The gospel is alive, life-changing and dynamic as it works in us and flows out to others. With the incisiveness of a surgeon's scalpel, God's Word reveals who we are and what we are not. It discerns what is in us, both good and evil. The demands of God's Word require decisions!

We must not only listen to the Word, but we must also allow it to shape our lives. The gospel flows don't let it pass you by! It is the absence of the gospel preached that allows people to grow stagnate in the pool of indecision and spiritual death! (see Hebrews 4:12).

The dilemma

This dilemma caused by this vast accepted shallowness was very obvious in much of the American church at the outset of the COVID-19 two years ago and remains dead to this day. The gospel means that we have been set free from the bondage of Satan, sin, and death and have been brought into the glorious light of freedom *in Christ*. However our lives were defined prior to Christ, by worldly criteria no longer! Gospel-centered church happens when we are confronted with the reality that our life is not our own, it was bought with a price. The grace that purchased our freedom didn't come cheap – it was costly grace! The gospel is central to all of human existence:

Therefore remember that at one time you were Gentiles in the flesh, called "the uncircumcision" by what is called the circumcision, which is made in the flesh by hand – remember that you were at that time separated from Christ, alienated from the commonwealth of Israel and strangers to the **covenants of promise,** *having no hope and without God in the world.* **But now in Christ Jesus you who once were far off have been brought near by the blood of Christ.**

For he himself is our peace, who has made us both one and has broken down in his flesh the dividing wall of hostility **by abolishing the law of commandments expressed in the ordinances,** *that he might* **create in himself one new man in place of the two,** *so making peace, and might reconcile us both to God in one body through the cross, thereby killing the hostility. And* **he came and preached peace to you who were far off** *and to them who were near. For through him we both have access in one Spirit to the Father. So then you are no longer strangers and aliens, but you are fellow citizens with the saints and members of the household of God* (Ephesians 2:11-22). Emphasis mine throughout.

Before the foundation of the world

Through Christ in the New Covenant with Him, God redeems and reconciles a people unto Himself. He takes those whom the book of Ephesians calls dead, estranged, lost, and alienated – and He engrafts them into His grand gospel plan, making them adopted sons and daughters in the family of God. Clearly we see in the gospel how He brought us from death to life and into His eternal plan. Paul writes that when God reconciles us to Himself, He calls us out of death and darkness into life and light.

Now that we have died with Christ, we believe that we shall also live with Him. Paul is not speaking of our living with Christ throughout eternity, but also that all who have died with Christ, will live a life here, that is fully consistent with His holiness. I had it backward! I had thought victory over sin was only for the strong, but I came to understand through the richness of the gospel flow in me that my being a victorious Christian has nothing to do with the greatness of my efforts. It all rests on the One who lives in me.

With all my heart I wanted to live for God and do what was right in His eyes, but almost daily I was frustrated by not being able to stop sinning! Jay Leach

---

As a result of my personal struggles, I eventually came to believe that fighting sin was what Christians do. We fight sin, hope we win, fail again, repent. An old worldly song was titled, "Only the Strong Survive." Everything was about "resisting the devil" and "striving against sin." But none of it helped me overcome the tiredness and fatigue continually fighting a [daily] battle that I could never seem to win.

The Christian can come to a place where his or her besetting sins are overcome *by the power of the Holy Spirit* never to trouble them again. Praise God!

He makes those who were once strangers and aliens sons and daughters. Again, the dilemma is not that our people are not willing to go deeper, but that we only lead them shallow water. As shepherd pastors we have the privilege and responsibility to move our people to deeper transformation [sanctification/ maturity] in Christ.

Our ability to accomplish this is only as limited as our understanding of the gospel. A church where the gospel is stagnant will always have the stench of death. Likewise, a community where the gospel is static is not a source of life. Amen!

STUDY GUIDE: CHAPTER 17 THE GOSPEL FLOW

1. When considering the importance of clean water in natural life; how much more crucial is to be _____, water of the Word (the gospel flow).

2. Many pastors have built a _____ gospel in the minds and hearts of their people.

3. People desire immersion deeper into Christ and obedience to His Word, but all the church offers is _____.

4. The structure of the ministry reflects the priority given to deeper _____ _____ relationships and church activities.

5. We must not only study the Word, but we must let it _____ or lives.

6. Clearly we see in the New Covenant, how God with Christ redeems and reconciles _____ _____ unto _____.

7. A church where the _____ is _____ will always have a stench of death.

CHAPTER EIGHTEEN
THE PEOPLE OF GOD

*"Therefore, from now on, we regard no one according to the flesh. Even though we have known Christ according to the flesh, yet now we know Him thus no longer. Therefore, if anyone is in Christ, he is a new creation; old things have passed away; behold, all things have become new. Now all things are of God, who has reconciled us to Himself through Jesus Christ, **and has given us the ministry of reconciliation,** that is, that God was in Christ reconciling the world to Himself, not imputing their trespasses to them, and has committed to us the word of reconciliation. Now then, we are ambassadors for Christ, we implore you on Christ's behalf, be reconciled to God. For He made who knew no sin to be sin for us, that we might become the righteousness of God in Him"* (2 Cor. 5:16-21 NKJV). Emphasis added.

I t is very interesting how the church has existed from her inception and moved in the world, since her birth. Throughout the New

Testament, the Holy Spirit comes upon a people and the gospel takes root in such a way that it transforms that community and begins to flow beyond that group to the world around them (Acts 2:42-47; 2 Cor. 5:16-21). All of us who today holding faith in Jesus Christ are a part of this gospel flow. When considering building toward a gospel-centered church, we must talk about biblical shepherd leadership.

If our desire is to see the message of the gospel go forward and transform the hearts and lives of the people in our churches, which would be a proper mindset for all preachers and teachers as we emerge from the closures and other obstacles caused by the COVID-19 epidemic. Prior to the epidemic many people were concerned about how messy the church in America had become during the past 150 years.

What would the early church fathers say if they could see us now? They may ask, where is the joy, love and generosity spoken of in the book of Acts? If the bride of Christ is functioning as He designed us to, we can be a deep, spiritual, life-giving group of God's people running to restore what is broken.

Instead of fostering disunity and pain – we can dwell together in unity, joy, and redemption! My purpose in writing this book is to attempt to show from Scripture what a healthy Spirit-filled, shepherd-led, disciple-making church looks like. This book is fueled by a passion. We at the Bread of Life Ministries are giving our lives to help Christians and local churches recover biblical health. I really believe it can happen and is already happening around the world. Certainly, church should not be boring or painful – knowing that it can be thrilling and life-giving, because we were designed by a life-giving God.

Our role as pastors in the church is to equip and serve the people of God to be the church to one another. From discipline to benevolence – through equipping our leaders to shepherd well. We can push ministry (discipling, and evangelism) down into the entire body of believers. "Making disciples" has been placed on the back shelf and out of sight (claimed by many to be obsolete or outdated) in many of the local churches in this country. I think it's time to sound the alarm from the pulpits across the land – that we had better get the church back on track and *restore* the faith, love, and obedience to our Lord and Savior, Jesus Christ. For example, discipling is a command of Christ for His church to "obey!"

The people of God are a called-out people and should play a primary role in discipleship, and community (church), the primary place where that discipleship takes place. Christ's command to "Go!" is for all of the church (every member ministry).

"You are either already in or soon to be engaged in church-life recovery!" Jay Leach

---

When it comes to the mission God has given to the Church (see Matthew 28:18-20). You don't have to settle for the mundane church life. Think of who and what the Church is *in* Christ. The Church is a supernatural and miraculous *movement of God* that we got swept up in. Although God alone saved me. He used the people of God to administer the gospel by the power of His Holy Spirit. As I mentioned earlier, the gospel mission of God pushes forward through the people of God. Before the pandemic there were two issues that every pastor and church leader across this nation have had to face:

- There are not enough shepherd pastors to keep up with the demands.
- The second issue is the fact that groups seldom want to multiply (status quo).

If we aren't careful, we could suffer dissipation of the discipling culture in the church through negligence in a couple of generations. The forward movement of a gospel-driven church is made up of disciples, who make disciples who in turn make disciples – the process continues throughout the generations. Many local churches minimize the expectations of leaders and establish the barrier of entry into that role as low as possible – thus, the gospel flow decreases.

The church or ministry's depth and direction will rise and fall depending on the men and women to whom you give the responsibility of leading. In an earlier chapter I contrasted leaders and shepherds. Perhaps it would be fruitful go over that portion again. Biblical leadership is the shepherd model at all levels (paid and lay leaders). The shepherd model leads from the heart by the Spirit and the Word, while leaders in general lead from their head an much learning (leaning to their own understanding). Certainly, there is a vast difference.

It has been said, "The importance you place on the role at the front end will greatly affect what the leader accomplishes at the backend."

There is a common denominator that links every church. No matter in what denomination, city, country, or context the church exists:

- All churches are made up of people! Somewhere along the line sin, and suffering will surface in the church or group and the shepherd leader will have to wade into the waters and deal with it in the church.

The post moral age

If there are no standards, there is nothing to enforce. Is it possible that this perspective has found its way into the church? Listen to Albert Mohler concerning this point… the modern secular worldview has wrought destruction within the church as well. The modern attempt to dominate truth has given way within sectors of the church to the post-modern rejection of truth itself. Indeed, in many denominations and churches, notions of orthodoxy and heresy have become "conceptual emptiness." The boundaries have vanished. The very possibility of heresy is dismissed in many circles within mainline Protestantism, and many evangelicals seem to have no better grasp of the moral imperative to honor the truth and to oppose error.[46] If the boundaries have vanished between truth and falsehood in doctrine, it turns doctrine into a "conceptual emptiness," it follows that the boundaries of right and wrong *praxis* have given way to a "moral emptiness" as well.

The *will* to draw lines of right and wrong clearly and authoritatively has disappeared and a newly found *will* has been found to stand *against* those who would oppose immorality "In our day of diversity and tolerance, where God the Creator has been dethroned, denouncing error has become the ultimate unpardonable sin (to man). Opposition to anything that others hold dear makes a bigot and a hate monger. The lines for discipline have been drawn, the leaders of churches that advocate certain *diverse* lifestyles are in no position to discipline members who engage in such lifestyles. If God has been dethroned, how effective are Scriptural standards? If the standards are self-generated, there is no ground upon which the church can stand to exercise discipline. As a result of these conditions litigation by congregants against pastors who may well be exercising their biblical responsibilities of church discipline.

---

[46] Albert R. Mohler, "The Truth of God's Word," in *The Formal Papers of the Alliance of Confessing Evangelicals* (April 17-20, 1996). 3.

Rethink everything you thought you knew

Those God has saved are called *to be the church,* not *go to* church. This distinction is vitally important. The church consists of all those who entered into the New Covenant that Jesus instituted by putting trust in Him and surrendering their all to Him. Yet, the church is much more than a *collection of individuals.* Rather when a person surrenders to Christ, the Holy Spirit of God incorporates them into a living organism that the New Testament calls "the body of Christ" (see 1 Cor. 12:27) Each newly incorporated individual is *organically related* to the other members of the body of Christ the way a person's hand is related to their arm, in other words, each member of the body of Christ is related to every other member (brothers and sisters) as part of a single, living organism (church family). This is difficult for many in the Western culture to grasp, largely because our culture is determinedly individualistic.[47]

Americans tend to define individuals *over and against others* rather than in relationship to others. We thus tend to define individuals that comprise a given social group (family, church, nation) as more real than the social group itself. Thus, individuals can join and leave a group with little effect on the individual or the social group.

---

[47] Assessed 12/16/21, http//the free dictionary.com/browse/individualistic. Philosophy of or relating to a belief that all actions are determined by or for the benefit of the individual, not society as a whole. The attempt to construct a new social order on the basis of individualistic doctrine was bound to fail, because the shared customs and practices that make up the common life of society are too valuable.

Of course, this is far from the Bible's view. The Bible views individuals and social groups as equally real biblically speaking, individuals and social groups are two sides of the same coin. Who we are individually is inextricably associated with *who we belong to*. This is why the Bible sometimes treat families, tribes, nations, even the whole human race as though they were single individuals.

There is an important sense in which all humans formed a single organic entity **"in Adam"** and now are being formed into a new, redeemed, single organic entity **"in Christ."** *"For as in Adam all die, even so in Christ all shall be made alive"* (1 Cor. 15:22 NKJV).

Paul also adds his perspective when he speaks of the church. When an individual surrenders to Christ and becomes part of God's bride, they become organically united with other disciples. The idea of a disciple being unattached to the body of Christ is unheard of in the New Testament. To be "in Christ" means one is part of the body over which Christ is Head."

> *"And He is before all things, and in Him all things exist. And He is the head of the body, the church, who is the beginning, the firstborn from the dead, that in all things He may have the preeminence"* (Col. 1:18 NKJV).

From a New Testament perspective, a Christian can no more live unattached to the body of Christ presuppose followers of Jesus are sharing life together in deep ways. With the New Testament teaching that we are members of the body of Christ, we should understand that it's assuming we will be participating in churches that are cultivating deep and sincere relationships. In my book *Drawn Away*, there are over fifty *"one another statements"* and *"commands"* from the New Testament which call the people of God to a special kind of life together.[48]

---

[48] Jay R. Leach, *Drawn Away* (Trafford Publishing 2012) 144-147

These statements are very important to God, since He speaks of them so frequently! I call them "One another Ministries." Jesus exhorted His disciples,

> *"A new commandment I give to you, that you love one another; even as I have loved you, that you also love one another. By this all men will know that you are My disciples, if you have love for one another"* (John 13:34-35 NKJV).

This is quite challenging [but not impossible through the Holy Spirit] for the largely individualistic Church today.

Members of One Bod

As Christians, we are made righteous and holy in Jesus alone. The Book of Corinthians tells us that, having been sanctified, we are called to live holy lives. Holy living requires that we rely *fully* on the Lord's wisdom and not on the wisdom of the world. We are able to understand and discern God's ways by the Holy Spirit. Likewise, the Spirit empowers us to live as God's people, holy, and set apart to Him. While individual relationship with Jesus will always be vital, we must also see ourselves as living members of Christ's body, the church. We must move from *individualism* and begin again the gathering and function of local congregations and the church as a whole. We have one head, who is Christ, and one body, the Church. Renew your commitment to the local body of believers. Seek to build up the Church through your words, actions, and participation.

STUDY GUIDE: CHAPTER 18 THE PEOPLE OF GOD

1. Prior to COVID-19 many people were _____ about how _____ the church in America has become over the past 150 years.

2. Our role as shepherd pastors in the church is to _____ and _____ the people of God to be the church to _____ _____.

3. Two issues pastors and other church leaders across America have had to face are: 1) _____ _____ _____ pastors. 2) groups seldom want to _____.

4. There is a common denominator that links every church, no matter the denomination.

5. If the boundaries have vanished between truth and falsehood in doctrine, it turns doctrine into a "_____ _____."

6. Americans tend to define _____ over and against others rather than in _____ to others.

7. "...by this all men will know that you are _____ _____."

CHAPTER NINETEEN
PASTORAL VIGILANCE

"As I live, declares the Lord GOD, surely with a mighty hand and an outstretched arm and with wrath poured out I will be a king over you" (Ezekiel 3, 33 ESV).

"Pay careful attention to yourselves and to all the flock, in which the Holy Spirit has made you overseers, to care for the church of God, which he obtained with his own blood" (Acts 20:28 ESV).

Today, guarding God's flock of believers from spiritual danger is one of the most neglected pastoral responsibilities in the church. In addition to commissioning spiritual watchmen to watch over His flock by directing them into *righteousness* and *truth*, God has charged these watchmen to protect the flock from doctrinal and personal sin. Ezekiel 3, 33 and Acts 20 provide explicit instructions on the why's and how's for being a pastoral watchman. For the past three or four decades, much has been discussed and written about an apostolic reformation. If anything positive come out of this coronavirus season, I pray that we would take a look at the recent moves of God (the Azusa Street revivals 1906 and beyond) and His *present desires* that for one reason or another, the church in this nation has determined to be mere recommendations and not commands.

I mention Azusa revivals because I believe that much of the body of Christ has missed the opportunity to really allow the Holy Spirit to move freely to reinstitute the power of Pentecost (the New Covenant) throughout the United States and the West. Undoubtedly, a short time passed 2000 years ago when the Holy Spirit was sent to the body of Christ at Pentecost and Jude and other apostles began appealing for the people to *"Contend for the faith that was once delivered to the saints"* (Jude 3, 4 ESV). For certain people *"have crept in unnoticed ... who pervert the grace of God into sensuality and deny our only Master and Lord, Jesus Christ."*

What are we to do personally?

Today, false teachers of unbiblical ethical standards, some of them even claim to have the Spirit, threaten the godly commitment of the brethren. However, God's *power* is able to keep us from falling. But *our* responsibility is to **1)** build ourselves up through the truth of God's Word, **2)** praying in the Holy Spirit and **3)** to anticipate our final salvation. The Spirit and the Scriptures are our resource. At the same time, we are to be vigilant and vocal in warning those who are being swayed by false doctrine, and humanistic philosophies so prevalent today. The corruption of "the truth" is found in self-centeredness, unloving behavior, immoral or sensual lifestyles, and in distorted or deceitful teaching.

The Holy Spirit in action

The Holy Spirit causes biblical teaching to come alive, so that the Christian community is built up in its "most holy faith," that is, in the apostolic teaching (see v. 20). The sensual persons are still a part of the church today (v. 12). From the earliest days of the church to this day not only teaching false doctrine but were gathering around themselves a faction within the church (much like Korah in v.11), an elitist group who were deceived into thinking they were the more spiritual.

There have always been those who attempt to *divert* God's people from their main purpose. Whether angels or men, God knows how to deal with the rebellious, but believers are warned not to participate with any such persons. The wicked appeals to the lusts of the eye, lusts of the flesh, and to inordinate pride. They will pretend to love God, appear to do good works, but on close examination they are fruitless as the fig tree, Jesus cursed. The godly wise will be able to identify those whose object is to be god, rather than to serve God. In an earlier section, I noted that, in these last days, Satan has turned up the heat on humanity, because he has but a short time. Additionally, it will take a deeply spiritual heart to know how to counter those who are deep into evil without being contaminated. We hate the sin, but still love the sinner.

Beware and reject anyone who teaches that grace is God's permission to "sin!" – Jay Leach

---

Keeping the church on track

The goal of any changes must be a return to the church's biblical roots if it is to ever regain its former glory. We must insure first of all that God's appointed shepherds who keep watch over His flock be one of the first areas of consideration.

The apostle Paul laid out the basic task of a shepherd with these words:

> *"And He Himself gave some to be apostles, some prophets, some evangelists, and some pastors and teachers, for the equipping of the saints for the work of ministry, for the edifying of the body of Christ, till we all come to the unity of the faith, and of the knowledge of the Son of God, to a perfect man, to the measure of the stature of the fulness of Christ; that we no longer be children, tossed to and fro and carried about with every wind of doctrine by the trickery of men, in the cunning craftiness of deceitful plotting, but, speaking the truth in love, may grow up in all things into Him who is the head – Christ – from whom the whole body, joined and knit together by what every joint supplies, according to the effective working by which every part does its share, causes growth of the body for the edifying of itself in love"* (Eph. 4:11-16 NKJV).

The true shepherd

I say again, the biblical approach to keeping the church in order during these tumultuous last days requires some change, but changes should be a return to the church's biblical roots. To keep from trying to fix what is not broken, there are certain foundational specifics that must be in place. The true shepherd is key in this inspection to insure:

- The **first Cornerstone** is still in place (see Ephesians 2:20; 1 Peter 2:4-8).
- That the church still rests on the **beginning foundation** (see 1 Cor. 3:11; Eph. 2:20).
- That we are using approved **building materials** (see 1 Peter 2:5).

- That we have the right **builders** (see 1 Cor. 3:9).
- That we used the right **leadership** (see Eph. 4:11-13).
- That the initial **standards** of quality control are still in place (see Eph. 4:13-16).
- That we are working from the **original blueprint** (see 2 Tim. 3:16-17).

Additionally, if the church is to win over false teaching and sin, the shepherd must provide positive, truthful, leadership to the flock. In leading the flock down the path of righteousness, the shepherd also watches for, warns, and even rescues the stray who has been enticed by false teaching and alluring sin. One cannot shepherd the flock with credibility without providing corrective oversight of watching and warning.

We must follow the example of Christ, who rightfully called the Pharisees blind guides, serpents, and whitewashed tombs (see Matthew 23). God's spiritual sentinels must be forthright in their challenges and strongly confront those who would maliciously usurp the true shepherd's tasks, and in so doing, lead Christ's flock astray.

To the Eastern shepherd, vigilance was a cardinal virtue. The shepherd could not indulge in periods of drowsiness, for the enemy was always close by. Only by their alertness could the enemy be extracted. There were many kinds of enemies, all of them fierce and sly in different ways. At certain seasons of the year there were fierce storms and swollen streams, which swiftly overflowed their banks. Swift action was necessary in order to escape destruction.

There were bears, wolves, and other vicious and more subtle animals. There were enemies in the air, birds of prey ever soaring ready to swoop down upon a lamb. And then, most dangerous of all, were human – robbers, wild bandits, who made a business of robbing sheepfolds and murdering shepherds. Ezekiel, Jerimiah, Isaiah, and Habakkuk called the shepherds watchmen set to warn and save!

Vigilance, without question, begins in the pulpit, but it goes far beyond that. Watching over the flock as a body does not preclude our watching over the congregation as individual Christians. Strong pulpit ministry has always been the backbone of shepherding.

"Only if pastors first guard themselves, will they be able to guard the sheep. Only if pastors first tend to their own spiritual life, will they be able to tend the flock of God."[49] John Stott

---

Pastoral oversight includes a strong emphasis on watching carefully for lurking spiritual danger according to the following sampling of New Testament exhortations:

- Then He charged them, saying, "Take heed, beware of the leaven of the Pharisees and the leaven of Herod" (Mark 8:15 NKJV).
- "Beware of the scribes, who desire to go around in long robes, love greetings in the marketplaces, the best seats in the synagogues, and the best places at feasts" (Luke 20:46).
- "Beware of dogs, beware of evil workers, beware of the mutilation!" (Phil. 3:2 NKJV).
- "Be sober, be vigilant, because your adversary the devil walks about like a roaring lion, seeking whom he may devour" (1 Peter 5:8 NKJV).
- "Look to yourselves, that we do not lose those things we worked for, but that we may receive a full reward" (2 John 2:8 NKJV).

---

[49] John Stott In "Ideals of Pastoral Ministry," *Bibliobeca Sacra* 146, no. 581 (January–March 1989): 11

Twenty-first century shepherd/ pastoring

The early church took these biblical instructions seriously. The twofold responsibility to reach the lost with the gospel and to watch over the saints continues to the *present*. Paul's address to the elders of the Ephesian church brings together the most explicit and complete instruction on spiritual leadership given to a New Testament church.

He relied heavily on the imagery and ideas of Ezekiel 3 and 33. The watchman theme extended itself far beyond Ezekiel. Not only was Paul a vigilant sentinel, but he commanded the elders of Ephesus to do likewise. At least five features support the close parallel between Ezekiel 3, 33, and Acts 20:

- Both Ezekiel and the Ephesians elders were appointed by God. *"I have appointed you a watchman"* (Ezekiel 3:17). *"The Holy Spirit has made overseers"* (Acts 20:28). The commission in both resulted from God's direct call to ministry.
- The task assigned to both essentially involved vigilant oversight. Both "watchman" in Ezekiel 3:16 and is translated "overseer" in Acts 20:28. Both prophet and shepherd pastor are accountable to God as a spiritual sentry responsible to warn of impending danger. Paul warned the Ephesian elders in Acts 20:28-31).
- The watchman in both passages is assigned to deliver God's Word as His warning. What proved true of Ezekiel (2:7; 3:17; 33:7) also marked Paul's ministry (Acts 20:20-21, 27). They both *delivered the Word of God without compromise!* That is why the apostle commended the elders to the Word of God's grace, which would be their message likewise (v. 32).
- The watchman had a word for both the *unrighteous* (Ezek. 3:18-19; 33:8-9) and the *righteous* (3:20-21). Paul preached repentance to both Jew and Gentile (Acts 20:21) and the whole

purpose of God to the church and to watch over the saints continues to the present.

Refuting Error

Paul wrote Titus that an overseer: "He must hold firm to the trustworthy word as taught, so that he may be able to give instruction in sound doctrine and also to rebuke those who contradict it" (Titus 1:9 ESV). To exhort and not to refute amounts to spiritual insubordination, even gross disobedience, and dereliction of duty.

John Stott exposed and confronted the growing negligence of late twentieth century shepherds in their failure to watch for and confront doctrinal error:

> This emphasis is unpopular today. It is frequently said that we must always be positive in their teaching, never negative. But those who say this have either not read the New Testament or having read it, they disagree with it. For the Lord Jesus and His apostles gave the example and even set forth the obligation to be negative in refuting error.

Is it possible that the neglect of this ministry is one of the major causes of theological confusion in the church today? To be sure, theological controversy is distasteful to sensitive spirits and has its spiritual dangers. Woe to those who enjoy it! But it cannot conscientiously be avoided. If, when false teaching arises, Christian leaders sit idly by and do nothing or turn tail and flee, they will earn the terrible epithet "hireling" who care nothing for Christ's flock.

Is it right to abandon His sheep and leave them defenseless against the wolves to be like "sheep without a shepherd?" Is it right to be content to see the flock scattered and individual sheep torn to pieces? Is it to be said of believers today, as it was of Israel, that "they were scattered for lack of a shepherd, and they became food for every beast of the field" (see Ezek. 34:5)?

Today even some of the fundamental doctrines of historic Christianity are being denied by some church leaders, including the infinite personality of the living God, the eternal deity, virgin birth, atoning death, bodily resurrection of Jesus, the Trinity, and the gospel of justification by grace alone through faith alone without any meritorious works. Shepherd pastors are to protect God's flock from error and seek to establish them in the truth.[50]

---

[50] Stott, "Ideals of Pastoral Ministry," 8.

STUDY GUIDE: CHAPTER 19 PASTORAL VIGILANCE

1. Today guarding God's flock of believers from spiritual danger is one of the most _____ _____ responsibilities in the church.

2. Today, false teachers of unbiblical ethical standards, threaten the godly commitment _____ the _____.

3. The goal of any changes must be a return to the church's biblical roots if it is to ever regain its _____ _____.

4. Church changes in these last days should be a _____to the church; biblical _____.

5. If pastors first guard themselves, then they can _____ the _____.

6. Strong pulpit ministry has always been the backbone of good shepherding.

7. Vigilance without question begins in the _____.

CHAPTER TWENTY
THE GLORIOUS CHURCH

"... Christ loved the church and gave Himself for her, that He might sanctify and cleanse her with the washing of water by the word" (Ephesians 5:25-26 NKJV).

We are a kingdom of priests; therefore we are called to pray. What is the ultimate goal of our prayers? That the true Church of God will stand victorious, complete, and ready for the return of Jesus. Many people associated with the Church today have absolutely no concept whatever of what it means to pray for or even talk about the glorious Church. Yet the Scripture says that the Church – the Bride of Christ – for whom He is coming, will be glorious!

In the New Testament Greek the word *doxo* means "glory." This is because it is God's glory which appears. From the word doxo we get the English word doxology, meaning "that which ascribes the glory of God." This brings us to the Church. Wherever the Scripture speaks of a glorious Church, it means a Church that is filled with God's glory, a church that has within it, the *manifest presence* of Almighty God. It is not a Church that is living on naked faith without any manifestation – but a Church that, through faith, has entered into a relationship with God where His visible, personal, and tangible presence *is with His people.* The Bible tells us that is the kind of Church that Jesus is coming back for.

Earlier we saw that Jesus redeemed the Church through His blood that He might sanctify her by the pure water of His Word. The blood and the water of the Word. Both are needed to make the Church ready for the coming of the Lord. I don't believe any Christian will be ready to meet the Lord who has not gone through the sanctifying, cleansing process of being taught and disciplined. The blood of Jesus is the redemptive price by which we were brought back out of the hands of Satan. Additionally, it is the job of the Holy Spirit to form the body of Christ.

> After we have been saved by the blood of Jesus, we are then sanctified and cleansed by the washing of the water by the Word.

Jesus' purpose in this is that He might present the Church to Himself as *"a glorious Church, not having spot or wrinkle or any such thing, but that she should be holy and without blemish"* (v. 27).

What constitutes the glorious church?

The first of three of seven traits of the glorious Church, the Church for which Christ will come are stated here. She is to be:

- Glorious – marked out by the manifest presence of God in her midst
- Holy
- Without blemish

Turn back to Ephesians 4, and we find the means by which the Church will be made ready for the coming of the Lord. Verse 11 speaks of the five-fold basic ministries given to the Church by Christ Himself: some to be apostles, some prophets, some evangelists, and some pastors and teachers, *"for the equipping [or perfecting] of the saints for the work of the ministry"* (v. 12).

The five-fold ministries should equip the saints to do the work of ministry for the edifying or building up of the Body of Christ. We find their over-arching goal: *"Till we all come to the unity of the faith and of the knowledge of the Son of God"* (v.13). The Greek word means not merely "knowledge" but "acknowledgment" – or the acknowledging of Jesus, the Son of God in His supreme authority over *every aspect of the Church,* then we will come into the *unity of the faith.*

Through this we are brought into two further parts of God's will: **1)** "to a perfect man," meaning a mature or full-grown man. And then, **2)** "to the measure of the stature of the fullness of Christ" here the word *"fullness"* is key. Until the Church of Jesus Christ, His Body, depicts Christ in all His fulness – in every aspect, in every grace, in every gift, in every ministry – that Church is not equipped to manifest Jesus Christ. In fact, we manifest to the world a small part of the totality of Christ. So we now have altogether the *seven traits* of the Church of God. Christ is preparing to make her ready for Himself that He may then take her to Himself. She shall be:

1. Glorious – filled with the manifest presence of God
2. Holy
3. Without blemish
4. Coming into the unity of the faith
5. Acknowledging Jesus Christ in His headship and Lordship and thus,
6. She will come into maturity and
7. Will manifest the fullness of Christ to the world

The *fullness of Christ*

I want us to realize that none of us can comprehend this fulness individually. I see individualism as a fierce enemy of God's people. Individualism continue to grow in this country. Sadly, the church is not going along unaffected by it. Many people in our churches have more friends outside than inside of the church, because our churches tend to be unfriendly. That should not be!

We cannot comprehend the fulness of God individually. It is only when we come together with other believers, all saints together that we are able to comprehend the totality of Jesus Christ. If we are going to experience the growth to Christlike maturity through which we need to patiently walk in the context of community – because I repeat, "it is impossible to experience any kind of growth on our own. Yet, many in the America's local churches are nervous about pursuing or participating in such in-depth relationships. Again, this is the results of institutionalized individualism.

However, we need to be in a covenant group with people we trust and with whom we can share our lives through good times and bad times. In covenant relationship, we say in essence, "I want to grow up in Christ with you. I want to laugh with you, cry with you, pray with you, share with you, study with you and grow with you, and grow up in Christ with you. I hope you want the same." want to experience His fulness together.

In Ephesians we find an excellent prayer of the apostle Paul for the Church:

> "For this reason I bow my knees to the Father of our
> Lord Jesus Christ, from whom the whole family in
> heaven and earth is named, that He would grant you,
> according to the riches of His glory, to be strengthened
> with might through His Spirit in the inner man, that

Christ may dwell in your hearts through faith; that you, being rooted and grounded in love, may be able to comprehend with all the saints what is the width and length and depth and height – to know the love of Christ which passes knowledge; that you may be filled with all the fullness of God."

Ephesians 3:14-19 NKJV

What a wonderful day that will be, when the Church of Jesus Christ will be the dwelling place of all the fullness of God. Ponder it, the totality of God in all His nature, in all His power, in all His aspects will be manifested in the Church. Only here and in Colossians 2:9, is the phrase *the fulness of God* used. There it reads,

"For in Him [Jesus] dwells all the fulness of the Godhead bodily" (v. 9 NKJV).

It is important to remember from the passage above, that the Spirit is the one who ministers the glory and makes it available. When the Holy Spirit has completed His work of forming the Body of Christ, the fullness of God will be manifested again. Do not ever think that this will happen to you alone. It is only as you come together with other believers into the unity of the faith and the acknowledging of Christ that you will be able to comprehend with all saints the width and the length, and the depth, and the height of God, and thus be filled with all the fulness of God. This is the purpose of God for the Body of Christ, the Church.

STUDY GUIDE: CHAPTER 20 THE GLORIOUS CHURCH

1. The Bride for which Christ is coming for shall _____ _____.

2. Jesus redeemed the church through His blood that He might sanctify her by the pure _____ of the _____.

3. Doxo means "glory." Glory means a church that has the manifest _____ of Almighty God.

4. The five-fold ministries are to equip the saints to do the work of ministry for the _____ or _____ _____ the body of Christ.

5. Study the seven traits of the Church of God is preparing to make her for Himself.

6. We cannot comprehend the _____ of _____ individually.

7. The Spirit is the one who minsters the _____and make it available.

A FINAL EMPHASIS

The only force capable of restoring the American Church in whatever areas she needs restoring is the Spirit of God animating the Word of God. Apart from a Spirit-enabled recovery and submission to the Word of God, there can be no hope of lasting restoration among any of God's people. Program and conventional leaders models may appear to work. Special events and spectacular productions may continue to inspire some. Dynamic sermons – may motivate for a while. But all of these things will soon fizzle out.

The only thing that brings lasting life and vigorous restoration to a church is the Holy Bible, rightly divided, preached, and taught, defining and Spiritually guided biblical shepherd-leadership, shaping and motivating the spiritual life of the body of Christ. That is because the Word itself is "living and powerful, and sharper than any two-edged sword, piercing even to the division of soul and spirit, and of joints and marrow, and is a discerner of the thoughts and intents of the heart" (Hebrews 4:12 NKJV).

But the church finds herself divided and torn on one point: What role has the Word of God (Bible) in giving the church its life?

Increasingly, more people are claiming that the Bible is not the Word of God, or that it merely contains the words of God, and that we need to release our grip on the Bible because it is culturally and socially bound, stuck in a first-century world with little or no relevance to our world today. Then there are those who teach from an open Bible regularly calling the people to believe what the Bible says and expect what the Bible promises. Yet seldom do they emphasize the Bible's priorities! Few approaches to the Bible today actually give the Word of God its central, life-giving place in the church.

In fact, due to our silence, much of the church is looking to secular disciplines for life and practices. Rather than allow the Word of God to upset their traditional and inherited mores and dreams that tomorrow will be yesterday. Who will yield to the Spirit today and say to the Lord, "here am I send me?" For much of the church today, our battles and inspiration comes from the pages of books, the sermons of preachers, and in the classrooms that train future servants of the church – unaware of the fight raging day in and day out for the souls of the people. Many are satisfied that assuming the best of all the leaders and teachers, thinking that the use of the same language and words mean agreement among all.

Be assured that no restoration comes easily or cheaply. Nor does it come without fervent Spirit-led prayer, diligence in study, earnestness in preaching and teaching, salvation and transformation, wisdom and risks in leadership. Unless we are willing to let the devil's disciples overrun us, we need to heed the Bible's call to watch, to wake from our sleep, and repent, and return to the work of our first love (see Revelation 2:2-7). The church's life depends on it:

- We cannot fear man and hope for the Lord to send restoration. We must fear God and God alone.
- We cannot expect restoration while *failing* to God, love God's Word, love God's people, and love our neighbors and enemies.

- We cannot serve our traditions, and hope God will do a new thing in the church.

We cannot hope to see God's glory while we put on shows for church members and seek the praises of men. God's glory cannot be faked, performed, programmed, bought, or ignored (think it will just go away), the devil has fooled some to think that growing ethnic and racial hatred are exceptions to the rule. So-called perpetuation of separation, individualism, and secularism are making a mockery of this great nation as we bash other countries concerning human rights issues and other atrocities for which we ourselves are guilty. I pray that our nation and the American Church within her will repent and fervently pray concerning these silent issues of the church (see 2 Chronicles 7:14).

We must stand on the Word of God and realize that the "new thing" is actually an "old thing," the thing that was always true – God restores by His Spirit and His Word!

Signs and wonders

The denial of the Spirit, Spiritual gifts and graces in the local churches has really weakened their very purpose for existence. Many are merely producing spectators rather than Spirit-filled disciples. Therefore, the foundational infrastructures of many our local churches have faded away, allowing the sheep to wander at will. Like the culture outside, the church culture inside has determined that it is up to each individual to determine his or her way. Jesus made it clear, "Without Me you can do nothing." "So Christ Himself gave the apostles, prophets, the evangelists, the pastors and teachers, to equip His people for works of service, so that the body of Christ may be built up *until* we reach unity in the faith (see Jude 3), and in the knowledge of the Son of God and become mature, attaining to the whole measure of the fulness of Christ" (Ephesians 4:11-13 NIV). The *"until"* gives the duration of the fivefold offices. Until Jesus returns, the function is to continue, so are all the offices or ministries needed to bring about those functions. The operation of the gifts of the Spirit serves as the *means of accomplishing the goals of* verse 13.

Jesus declares in John's gospel, *"Very truly I tell you, whoever believes in me will do even greater things than these, because I am going to the Father"* (John 14:12 NIV). This should reveal (to all) that it is the **"whoever believes"** of John 14:12 who do the work of the Lord. Those who believe receives salvation and will receive the Holy Spirit (see John 7:37-39), who will enable them to exercise the (gifts of the Spirit) Jesus pours out upon them.

Note the following New Testament passages that indicate the Spiritual gifts were not for the apostles use only: Romans 12:3-8; Galatians 3:5; Ephesians 3:20-21; 1 Thessalonians 1:5-8; 2 Thessalonians 1:11; 1 Peter 4:7-12. Again, as in all of the references in this section, the ministry gifts are to continue operating until Jesus' Second Coming.

In conclusion, the question is not whether the church is on life support or not. The question is and always has been: Will we believe God? Will the church remain faithful to the end, obeying all that Christ has commanded? If she does, then she just might see those new days of the Spirit's outpouring and restoration. The church of Jesus Christ has been and always will be *supernatural in nature*. There is no biblical evidence to support modern believers who subscribe it to a theology that relegates the miraculous power of God to the early church era only. Make no mistake it will only happen by the Spirit and the Word of God working in tandem. Let us believe God for a fresh release of His wonder-working restoration power! In Paul's second letter to the Thessalonian church he states,

> *"With this in mind, we constantly pray for you, that our God may count you worthy of His calling, and that by His power He may fulfill every good purpose of yours and every act prompted by your faith. We pray this so that the name of our Lord Jesus may be glorified in you, and you in Him, according to the grace of our God and the Lord Jesus Christ"* (2 Thessalonians 1:11-12 NIV). Emphasis mine.

Printed in the United States
by Baker & Taylor Publisher Services